THREE SISTERS

A Drama in Four Acts

ANTON CHEKHOV

Translated by
JULIUS WEST

CONTENTS

CHARACTERS

ANDREY SERGEYEVITCH PROSOROV

NATALIA IVANOVA (NATASHA), his fiancée, later
his wife (28)

His sisters:

OLGA

MASHA

IRINA

FEODOR ILITCH KULIGIN, high school teacher,
married to MASHA (20)

ALEXANDER IGNATEYEVITCH VERSHININ,
lieutenant-colonel in charge of a battery (42)

NICOLAI LVOVITCH TUZENBACH, baron,
lieutenant in the army (30)

VASSILI VASSILEVITCH SOLENI, captain

IVAN ROMANOVITCH CHEBUTIKIN, army doctor (60)

ALEXEY PETROVITCH FEDOTIK, sub-lieutenant

VLADIMIR CARLOVITCH RODE, sub-lieutenant

FERAPONT, door-keeper at local council offices, an old man

ANFISA, nurse (80)

ACT I

[In PROSOROV'S house. A sitting-room with pillars; behind is seen a large dining-room. It is midday, the sun is shining brightly outside. In the dining-room the table is being laid for lunch.

[OLGA, in the regulation blue dress of a teacher at a girl's high school, is walking about correcting exercise books; MASHA, in a black dress, with a hat on her knees, sits and reads a book; IRINA, in white, stands about, with a thoughtful expression.]

OLGA. It's just a year since father died last May the fifth, on your name-day, Irina. It was very cold then, and snowing. I thought I would never survive it, and you were in a dead faint. And now a year has gone by and we are already thinking about it without pain, and you are wearing a white dress and your face is happy. *[Clock strikes twelve]* And the clock struck just the same way then. *[Pause]* I remember that there was music at the funeral, and they fired a volley in the cemetery. He was a general in command of a brigade but there were few people present. Of course, it was raining then, raining hard, and snowing.

IRINA. Why think about it!

[BARON TUZENBACH, CHEBUTIKIN and SOLENI appear by the table in the dining-room, behind the pillars.]

OLGA. It's so warm to-day that we can keep the windows open, though the birches are not yet in flower. Father was put in command of a brigade, and he rode out of Moscow with us eleven years ago. I remember perfectly that it was early in May and that everything in Moscow was flowering then. It was warm too, everything was bathed in sunshine. Eleven years have gone, and I remember everything as if we rode out only yesterday. Oh, God! When I awoke this morning and saw all the light and the spring, joy entered my heart, and I longed passionately to go home.

CHEBUTIKIN. Will you take a bet on it?

TUZENBACH. Oh, nonsense.

[MASHA, lost in a reverie over her book, whistles softly.]

OLGA. Don't whistle, Masha. How can you! *[Pause]* I'm always having headaches from having to go to the High School every day and then teach till evening. Strange thoughts come to me, as if I were already an old woman. And really, during these four years that I have been working here, I have been feeling as if every day my strength and youth have been squeezed out of me, drop by drop. And only one desire grows and gains in strength...

IRINA. To go away to Moscow. To sell the house, drop everything here, and go to Moscow...

OLGA. Yes! To Moscow, and as soon as possible.

[CHEBUTIKIN and TUZENBACH laugh.]

IRINA. I expect Andrey will become a professor, but still, he won't want to live here. Only poor Masha must go on living here.

OLGA. Masha can come to Moscow every year, for the whole summer.

[MASHA is whistling gently.]

IRINA. Everything will be arranged, please God. *[Looks out of the window]* It's nice out to-day. I don't know why I'm so happy: I remembered this morning that it was my name-day, and I suddenly felt glad and remembered my childhood, when mother was still with us. What beautiful thoughts I had, what thoughts!

OLGA. You're all radiance to-day, I've never seen you look so lovely. And Masha is pretty, too. Andrey wouldn't be bad-looking, if he wasn't so stout; it does spoil his appearance. But I've grown old and very thin, I suppose it's because I get angry with the girls at school. To-day I'm free. I'm at home. I haven't got a headache, and I feel younger than I was yesterday. I'm only twenty-eight.... All's well, God is everywhere, but it seems to me that if only I were married and could stay at home all day, it would be even better. *[Pause]* I should love my husband.

TUZENBACH. *[To SOLENI]* I'm tired of listening to the rot you talk. *[Entering the sitting-room]* I forgot to say that Vershinin, our new lieutenant-colonel of artillery, is coming to see us to-day. *[Sits down to the piano.]*

OLGA. That's good. I'm glad.

IRINA. Is he old?

TUZENBACH. Oh, no. Forty or forty-five, at the very outside. *[Plays softly]* He seems rather a good sort. He's certainly no fool, only he likes to hear himself speak.

IRINA. Is he interesting?

TUZENBACH. Oh, he's all right, but there's his wife, his mother-in-law, and two daughters. This is his second wife. He pays calls and tells everybody that he's got a wife and two daughters. He'll tell you so here. The wife isn't all there, she does her hair like a flapper and gushes extremely. She talks philosophy and tries to commit suicide every now and again, apparently in order to annoy her husband. I should have left her long ago, but he bears up patiently, and just grumbles.

SOLENI. *[Enters with CHEBUTIKIN from the dining-room]* With one hand I can only lift fifty-four pounds, but with both hands I can lift 180, or even 200 pounds. From this I conclude that two men are not twice as strong as one, but three times, perhaps even more....

CHEBUTIKIN. *[Reads a newspaper as he walks]* If your hair is coming out... take an ounce of naphthaline and hail a bottle of spirit... dissolve and use daily.... *[Makes a note in his pocket diary]* When found make a note of! Not that I want it though.... *[Crosses it out]* It doesn't matter.

IRINA. Ivan Romanovitch, dear Ivan Romanovitch!

CHEBUTIKIN. What does my own little girl want?

IRINA. Ivan Romanovitch, dear Ivan Romanovitch! I feel as if I were sailing under the broad blue sky with great white birds around me. Why is that? Why?

CHEBUTIKIN. *[Kisses her hands, tenderly]* My white bird....

IRINA. When I woke up to-day and got up and dressed myself, I suddenly began to feel as if everything in this life was open to me, and that I knew how I must live. Dear Ivan Romanovitch, I know everything. A man must work, toil in the sweat of his brow, whoever he may be, for that is the meaning and object of his life, his happiness, his enthusiasm. How fine it is to be a workman who gets up at daybreak and breaks stones in the street, or a shepherd, or a schoolmaster, who teaches children, or an engine-driver on the railway.... My God, let alone a man, it's better to be an ox, or just a horse, so long as it can work, than a young woman who wakes up at twelve o'clock, has her coffee in bed, and then spends two hours dressing.... Oh it's awful! Sometimes when it's hot, your thirst can be just as tiresome as my need for work. And if I don't get up early in future and work, Ivan Romanovitch, then you may refuse me your friendship.

CHEBUTIKIN. *[Tenderly]* I'll refuse, I'll refuse....

OLGA. Father used to make us get up at seven. Now Irina wakes at seven and lies and meditates about something till nine at least. And she looks so serious! *[Laughs.]*

IRINA. You're so used to seeing me as a little girl that it seems queer to you when my face is serious. I'm twenty!

TUZENBACH. How well I can understand that craving for work, oh God! I've never worked once in my life. I was born in Petersburg, a chilly, lazy place, in a family which never knew what work or worry meant. I remember that when I used to come home from my regiment, a footman used to have to pull off my boots while I fidgeted and my mother looked on in adoration and wondered why other people didn't see me in the same light. They shielded me from work; but only just in time! A new age is dawning, the people are marching on us all, a powerful, health-giving storm is gathering, it is drawing near, soon it will be upon us and it will drive away laziness, indifference, the prejudice against labour, and rotten dullness from our society. I shall work, and in twenty-five or thirty years, every man will have to work. Every one!

CHEBUTIKIN. I shan't work.

TUZENBACH. You don't matter.

SOLENI. In twenty-five years' time, we shall all be dead, thank the Lord. In two or three years' time apoplexy will carry you off, or else I'll blow your brains out, my pet.

[Takes a scent-bottle out of his pocket and sprinkles his chest and hands.]

CHEBUTIKIN. *[Laughs]* It's quite true, I never have worked. After I came down from the university I never stirred a finger or opened a book, I just read the papers.... *[Takes another newspaper out of his pocket]* Here we are.... I've learnt from the papers that there used to be one, Dobrolubov *[Note: Dobroluboy (1836-81), in spite of the shortness of his career, established himself as one of the classic literary critics of Russia]*, for instance, but what he wrote—I don't know... God only knows.... *[Somebody is heard tapping on the floor from below]* There.... They're calling me downstairs, somebody's come to see me. I'll be back in a minute... won't be long.... *[Exit hurriedly, scratching his beard.]*

IRINA. He's up to something.

TUZENBACH. Yes, he looked so pleased as he went out that I'm pretty certain he'll bring you a present in a moment.

IRINA. How unpleasant!

OLGA. Yes, it's awful. He's always doing silly things.

MASHA.

> "There stands a green oak by the sea.
> And a chain of bright gold is around it...
> And a chain of bright gold is around it...."

[Gets up and sings softly.]

OLGA. You're not very bright to-day, Masha. *[MASHA sings, putting on her hat]* Where are you off to?

MASHA. Home.

IRINA. That's odd....

TUZENBACH. On a name-day, too!

MASHA. It doesn't matter. I'll come in the evening. Good-bye, dear. *[Kisses MASHA]* Many happy returns, though I've said it before. In the old days when father was alive, every time we had a name-day, thirty or forty officers used to come, and there was lots of noise and fun, and to-day there's only a man and a half, and it's as quiet as a desert... I'm off... I've got the hump to-day, and am not at all cheerful, so don't you mind me. *[Laughs through her tears]* We'll have a talk later on, but good-bye for the present, my dear; I'll go somewhere.

IRINA. *[Displeased]* You are queer....

OLGA. *[Crying]* I understand you, Masha.

SOLENI. When a man talks philosophy, well, it is philosophy or at any rate sophistry; but when a woman, or two women, talk philosophy—it's all my eye.

MASHA. What do you mean by that, you very awful man?

SOLENI. Oh, nothing. You came down on me before I could say... help! *[Pause.]*

MASHA. *[Angrily, to OLGA]* Don't cry!

[Enter ANFISA and FERAPONT with a cake.]

ANFISA. This way, my dear. Come in, your feet are clean. *[To IRINA]* From the District Council, from Mihail Ivanitch Protopopov... a cake.

IRINA. Thank you. Please thank him. *[Takes the cake.]*

FERAPONT. What?

IRINA. *[Louder]* Please thank him.

OLGA. Give him a pie, nurse. Ferapont, go, she'll give you a pie.

FERAPONT. What?

ANFISA. Come on, gran'fer, Ferapont Spiridonitch. Come on. *[Exeunt.]*

MASHA. I don't like this Mihail Potapitch or Ivanitch, Protopopov. We oughtn't to invite him here.

IRINA. I never asked him.

MASHA. That's all right.

[Enter CHEBUTIKIN followed by a soldier with a silver samovar; there is a rumble of dissatisfied surprise.]

OLGA. *[Covers her face with her hands]* A samovar! That's awful! *[Exit into the dining-room, to the table.]*

IRINA. My dear Ivan Romanovitch, what are you doing!

TUZENBACH. *[Laughs]* I told you so!

MASHA. Ivan Romanovitch, you are simply shameless!

CHEBUTIKIN. My dear good girl, you are the only thing, and the dearest thing I have in the world. I'll soon be sixty. I'm an old man, a lonely worthless old man. The only good thing in me is my love for you, and if it hadn't been for that, I would have been dead long ago.... *[To IRINA]* My dear little girl, I've known you since the day of your birth, I've carried you in my arms... I loved your dead mother....

MASHA. But your presents are so expensive!

CHEBUTIKIN. *[Angrily, through his tears]* Expensive presents.... You really, are!... *[To the orderly]* Take the samovar in there.... *[Teasing]* Expensive presents!

[The orderly goes into the dining-room with the samovar.]

ANFISA. *[Enters and crosses stage]* My dear, there's a strange Colonel come! He's taken off his coat already. Children, he's coming here. Irina darling, you'll be a nice and polite little girl, won't you.... Should have lunched a long time ago.... Oh, Lord.... *[Exit.]*

TUZENBACH. It must be Vershinin. *[Enter VERSHININ]* Lieutenant-Colonel Vershinin!

VERSHININ. *[To MASHA and IRINA]* I have the honour to introduce myself, my name is Vershinin. I am very glad indeed to be able to come at last. How you've grown! Oh! oh!

IRINA. Please sit down. We're very glad you've come.

VERSHININ. *[Gaily]* I am glad, very glad! But there are three sisters, surely. I remember—three little girls. I forget your faces, but your father, Colonel Prosorov, used to have three little girls, I remember that perfectly, I saw them with my own eyes. How time does fly! Oh, dear, how it flies!

TUZENBACH. Alexander Ignateyevitch comes from Moscow.

IRINA. From Moscow? Are you from Moscow?

VERSHININ. Yes, that's so. Your father used to be in charge of a battery there, and I was an officer in the same brigade. *[To MASHA]* I seem to remember your face a little.

MASHA. I don't remember you.

IRINA. Olga! Olga! *[Shouts into the dining-room]* Olga! Come along! *[OLGA enters from the dining-room]* Lieutenant Colonel Vershinin comes from Moscow, as it happens.

VERSHININ. I take it that you are Olga Sergeyevna, the eldest, and that you are Maria... and you are Irina, the youngest....

OLGA. So you come from Moscow?

VERSHININ. Yes. I went to school in Moscow and began my service there; I was there for a long time until at last I got my battery and moved over here, as you see. I don't really remember you, I only remember that there used to be three sisters. I remember your father well; I have only to shut my eyes to see him as he was. I used to come to your house in Moscow....

OLGA. I used to think I remembered everybody, but...

VERSHININ. My name is Alexander Ignateyevitch.

IRINA. Alexander Ignateyevitch, you've come from Moscow. That is really quite a surprise!

OLGA. We are going to live there, you see.

IRINA. We think we may be there this autumn. It's our native town, we were born there. In Old Basmanni Road.... [They both laugh for joy.]

MASHA. We've unexpectedly met a fellow countryman. [Briskly] I remember: Do you remember, Olga, they used to speak at home of a "lovelorn Major." You were only a Lieutenant then, and in love with somebody, but for some reason they always called you a Major for fun.

VERSHININ. [Laughs] That's it... the lovelorn Major, that's got it!

MASHA. You only wore moustaches then. You have grown older! [Through her tears] You have grown older!

VERSHININ. Yes, when they used to call me the lovelorn Major, I was young and in love. I've grown out of both now.

OLGA. But you haven't a single white hair yet. You're older, but you're not yet old.

VERSHININ. I'm forty-two, anyway. Have you been away from Moscow long?

IRINA. Eleven years. What are you crying for, Masha, you little fool.... [Crying] And I'm crying too.

MASHA. It's all right. And where did you live?

VERSHININ. Old Basmanni Road.

OLGA. Same as we.

VERSHININ. Once I used to live in German Street. That was when the Red Barracks were my headquarters. There's an ugly bridge in between, where the water rushes underneath. One gets melancholy when one is alone there. [Pause] Here the river is so wide and fine! It's a splendid river!

OLGA. Yes, but it's so cold. It's very cold here, and the midges....

VERSHININ. What are you saying! Here you've got such a fine healthy Russian climate. You've a forest, a river... and birches. Dear, modest birches, I like them more than any other tree. It's good to live here. Only it's odd that the railway station should be thirteen miles away.... Nobody knows why.

SOLENI. I know why. [All look at him] Because if it was near it wouldn't be far off, and if it's far off, it can't be near. [An awkward pause.]

TUZENBACH. Funny man.

OLGA. Now I know who you are. I remember.

VERSHININ. I used to know your mother.

CHEBUTIKIN. She was a good woman, rest her soul.

IRINA. Mother is buried in Moscow.

OLGA. At the Novo-Devichi Cemetery.

MASHA. Do you know, I'm beginning to forget her face. We'll be forgotten in just the same way.

VERSHININ. Yes, they'll forget us. It's our fate, it can't be helped. A time will come when everything that seems serious, significant, or very important to us will be forgotten, or considered trivial. *[Pause]* And the curious thing is that we can't possibly find out what will come to be regarded as great and important, and what will be feeble, or silly. Didn't the discoveries of Copernicus, or Columbus, say, seem unnecessary and ludicrous at first, while wasn't it thought that some rubbish written by a fool, held all the truth? And it may so happen that our present existence, with which we are so satisfied, will in time appear strange, inconvenient, stupid, unclean, perhaps even sinful....

TUZENBACH. Who knows? But on the other hand, they may call our life noble and honour its memory. We've abolished torture and capital punishment, we live in security, but how much suffering there is still!

SOLENI. *[In a feeble voice]* There, there.... The Baron will go without his dinner if you only let him talk philosophy.

TUZENBACH. Vassili Vassilevitch, kindly leave me alone. *[Changes his chair]* You're very dull, you know.

SOLENI. *[Feebly]* There, there, there.

TUZENBACH. *[To VERSHININ]* The sufferings we see to-day—there are so many of them!—still indicate a certain moral improvement in society.

VERSHININ. Yes, yes, of course.

CHEBUTIKIN. You said just now, Baron, that they may call our life noble; but we are very petty.... *[Stands up]* See how little I am. *[Violin played behind.]*

MASHA. That's Andrey playing—our brother.

IRINA. He's the learned member of the family. I expect he will be a professor some day. Father was a soldier, but his son chose an academic career for himself.

MASHA. That was father's wish.

OLGA. We ragged him to-day. We think he's a little in love.

IRINA. To a local lady. She will probably come here to-day.

MASHA. You should see the way she dresses! Quite prettily, quite fashionably too, but so badly! Some queer bright yellow skirt with a wretched little fringe and a red bodice. And such a complexion! Andrey isn't in love. After all he has taste, he's simply making fun of us. I heard yesterday that she was going to marry Protopopov, the chairman of the Local Council. That would do her nicely.... *[At the side door]* Andrey, come here! Just for a minute, dear! *[Enter ANDREY.]*

OLGA. My brother, Andrey Sergeyevitch.

VERSHININ. My name is Vershinin.

ANDREY. Mine is Prosorov. *[Wipes his perspiring hands]* You've come to take charge of the battery?

OLGA. Just think, Alexander Ignateyevitch comes from Moscow.

ANDREY. That's all right. Now my little sisters won't give you any rest.

VERSHININ. I've already managed to bore your sisters.

IRINA. Just look what a nice little photograph frame Andrey gave me to-day. *[Shows it]* He made it himself.

VERSHININ. *[Looks at the frame and does not know what to say]* Yes.... It's a thing that...

IRINA. And he made that frame there, on the piano as well. *[Andrey waves his hand and walks away.]*

OLGA. He's got a degree, and plays the violin, and cuts all sorts of things out of wood, and is really a domestic Admirable Crichton. Don't go away, Andrey! He's got into a habit of always going away. Come here!

[MASHA and IRINA take his arms and laughingly lead him back.]

MASHA. Come on, come on!

ANDREY. Please leave me alone.

MASHA. You are funny. Alexander Ignateyevitch used to be called the lovelorn Major, but he never minded.

VERSHININ. Not the least.

MASHA. I'd like to call you the lovelorn fiddler!

IRINA. Or the lovelorn professor!

OLGA. He's in love! little Andrey is in love!

IRINA. *[Applauds]* Bravo, Bravo! Encore! Little Andrey is in love.

CHEBUTIKIN. *[Goes up behind ANDREY and takes him round the waist with both arms]* Nature only brought us into the world that we should love! *[Roars with laughter, then sits down and reads a newspaper which he takes out of his pocket.]*

ANDREY. That's enough, quite enough.... *[Wipes his face]* I couldn't sleep all night and now I can't quite find my feet, so to speak. I read until four o'clock, then tried to sleep, but nothing happened. I thought about one thing and another, and then it dawned and the sun crawled into my bedroom. This summer, while I'm here, I want to translate a book from the English....

VERSHININ. Do you read English?

ANDREY. Yes father, rest his soul, educated us almost violently. It may seem funny and silly, but it's nevertheless true, that after his death I began to fill out and get rounder, as if my body had had some great pressure taken off it. Thanks to father, my sisters and I know French, German, and English, and Irina knows Italian as well. But we paid dearly for it all!

MASHA. A knowledge of three languages is an unnecessary luxury in this town. It isn't even a luxury but a sort of useless extra, like a sixth finger. We know a lot too much.

VERSHININ. Well, I say! *[Laughs]* You know a lot too much! I don't think there can really be a town so dull and stupid as to have no place for a clever, cultured person. Let us suppose even that among the hundred thousand inhabitants of this backward and uneducated town, there are only three persons like yourself. It stands to reason that you won't be able to conquer that dark mob around you; little by little as you grow older you will be bound to give way and lose yourselves in this crowd of a hundred thousand human beings; their life will suck you up in itself, but still, you won't disappear having influenced nobody; later on, others like you will come, perhaps six of them, then twelve, and so on, until at last your sort will be in the majority. In two or three hundred years' time life on this earth will be unimaginably beautiful and wonderful. Mankind needs such a life, and if it is not ours to-day then we must look ahead for it, wait, think, prepare for it. We must see and know more than our fathers and grandfathers saw and knew. *[Laughs]* And you complain that you know too much.

MASHA. *[Takes off her hat]* I'll stay to lunch.

IRINA. *[Sighs]* Yes, all that ought to be written down.

[ANDREY has gone out quietly.]

TUZENBACH. You say that many years later on, life on this earth will be beautiful and wonderful. That's true. But to share in it now, even though at a distance, we must prepare by work....

VERSHININ. *[Gets up]* Yes. What a lot of flowers you have. *[Looks round]* It's a beautiful flat. I envy you! I've spent my whole life in rooms with two chairs, one sofa, and fires which always smoke. I've never had flowers like these in my life.... *[Rubs his hands]* Well, well!

TUZENBACH. Yes, we must work. You are probably thinking to yourself: the German lets himself go. But I assure you I'm a Russian, I can't even speak German. My father belonged to the Orthodox Church.... *[Pause.]*

VERSHININ. *[Walks about the stage]* I often wonder: suppose we could begin life over again, knowing what we were doing? Suppose we could use one life, already ended, as a sort of rough draft for another? I think that every one of us would try, more than anything else, not to repeat himself, at the very least he would rearrange his manner of life, he would make sure of rooms like these, with flowers and light... I have a wife and two daughters, my wife's health is delicate and so on and so on, and if I had to begin life all over again I would not marry.... No, no!

[Enter KULIGIN in a regulation jacket.]

KULIGIN. *[Going up to IRINA]* Dear sister, allow me to congratulate you on the day sacred to your good angel and to wish you, sincerely and from the bottom of my heart, good health and all that one can wish for a girl of your years. And then let me offer you this book as a present. *[Gives it to her]* It is the history of our High School during the last fifty years, written by myself. The book is worthless, and written because I had nothing to do, but read it all the same. Good day, gentlemen! *[To VERSHININ]* My name is Kuligin, I am a master of the local High School. *[Note: He adds that he is a Nadvorny Sovetnik (almost the same as a German Hofrat), an undistinguished civilian title with no English equivalent.]* *[To IRINA]* In this book you will find a list of all those who have taken the full course at our High School during these fifty years. *Feci quod potui, faciant meliora potentes.* *[Kisses MASHA.]*

IRINA. But you gave me one of these at Easter.

KULIGIN. *[Laughs]* I couldn't have, surely! You'd better give it back to me in that case, or else give it to the Colonel. Take it, Colonel. You'll read it some day when you're bored.

VERSHININ. Thank you. *[Prepares to go]* I am extremely happy to have made the acquaintance of...

OLGA. Must you go? No, not yet?

IRINA. You'll stop and have lunch with us. Please do.

OLGA. Yes, please!

VERSHININ. *[Bows]* I seem to have dropped in on your name-day. Forgive me, I didn't know, and I didn't offer you my congratulations. *[Goes with OLGA into the dining-room.]*

KULIGIN. To-day is Sunday, the day of rest, so let us rest and rejoice, each in a manner compatible with his age and disposition. The carpets will have to be taken up for the summer and put away till the winter... Persian powder or naphthaline.... The Romans were healthy because they knew both how to work and how to rest, they had *mens sana in corpore sano*. Their life ran along certain recognized patterns. Our director says: "The chief thing about each life is its pattern. Whoever loses his pattern is lost himself"—and it's just the same in our daily life. *[Takes MASHA by the waist, laughing]* Masha loves me. My wife loves me. And you ought to put the window curtains away with the carpets.... I'm feeling awfully pleased with life to-day. Masha, we've got to be at the director's at four. They're getting up a walk for the pedagogues and their families.

MASHA. I shan't go.

KULIGIN. *[Hurt]* My dear Masha, why not?

MASHA. I'll tell you later.... *[Angrily]* All right, I'll go, only please stand back.... *[Steps away.]*

KULIGIN. And then we're to spend the evening at the director's. In spite of his ill-health that man tries, above everything else, to be sociable. A splendid, illuminating personality. A wonderful man. After yesterday's committee he said to me: "I'm tired, Feodor Ilitch, I'm tired!" *[Looks at the clock, then at his watch]* Your clock is seven minutes fast. "Yes," he said, "I'm tired." *[Violin played off.]*

OLGA. Let's go and have lunch! There's to be a masterpiece of baking!

KULIGIN. Oh my dear Olga, my dear. Yesterday I was working till eleven o'clock at night, and got awfully tired. To-day I'm quite happy. *[Goes into dining-room]* My dear...

CHEBUTIKIN. *[Puts his paper into his pocket, and combs his beard]* A pie? Splendid!

MASHA. *[Severely to CHEBUTIKIN]* Only mind; you're not to drink anything to-day. Do you hear? It's bad for you.

CHEBUTIKIN. Oh, that's all right. I haven't been drunk for two years. And it's all the same, anyway!

MASHA. You're not to dare to drink, all the same. *[Angrily, but so that her husband should not hear]* Another dull evening at the Director's, confound it!

TUZENBACH. I shouldn't go if I were you.... It's quite simple.

CHEBUTIKIN. Don't go.

MASHA. Yes, "don't go...." It's a cursed, unbearable life.... *[Goes into dining-room.]*

CHEBUTIKIN. *[Follows her]* It's not so bad.

SOLENI. *[Going into the dining-room]* There, there, there....

TUZENBACH. Vassili Vassilevitch, that's enough. Be quiet!

SOLENI. There, there, there....

KULIGIN. *[Gaily]* Your health, Colonel! I'm a pedagogue and not quite at home here. I'm Masha's husband.... She's a good sort, a very good sort.

VERSHININ. I'll have some of this black vodka.... *[Drinks]* Your health! *[To OLGA]* I'm very comfortable here!

[Only IRINA and TUZENBACH are now left in the sitting-room.]

IRINA. Masha's out of sorts to-day. She married when she was eighteen, when he seemed to her the wisest of men. And now it's different. He's the kindest man, but not the wisest.

OLGA. *[Impatiently]* Andrey, when are you coming?

ANDREY. *[Off]* One minute. *[Enters and goes to the table.]*

TUZENBACH. What are you thinking about?

IRINA. I don't like this Soleni of yours and I'm afraid of him. He only says silly things.

TUZENBACH. He's a queer man. I'm sorry for him, though he vexes me. I think he's shy. When there are just the two of us he's quite all right and very good company; when other people are about he's rough and hectoring.

Don't let's go in, let them have their meal without us. Let me stay with you. What are you thinking of? *[Pause]* You're twenty. I'm not yet thirty. How many years are there left to us, with their long, long lines of days, filled with my love for you....

IRINA. Nicolai Lvovitch, don't speak to me of love.

TUZENBACH. *[Does not hear]* I've a great thirst for life, struggle, and work, and this thirst has united with my love for you, Irina, and you're so beautiful, and life seems so beautiful to me! What are you thinking about?

IRINA. You say that life is beautiful. Yes, if only it seems so! The life of us three hasn't been beautiful yet; it has been stifling us as if it was weeds... I'm crying. I oughtn't.... *[Dries her tears, smiles]* We must work, work. That is why we are unhappy and look at the world so sadly; we don't know what work is. Our parents despised work....

[Enter NATALIA IVANOVA; she wears a pink dress and a green sash.]

NATASHA. They're already at lunch... I'm late... *[Carefully examines herself in a mirror, and puts herself straight]* I think my hair's done all right.... *[Sees IRINA]* Dear Irina Sergeyevna, I congratulate you! *[Kisses her firmly and at length]* You've so many visitors, I'm really ashamed.... How do you do, Baron!

OLGA. *[Enters from dining-room]* Here's Natalia Ivanovna. How are you, dear! *[They kiss.]*

NATASHA. Happy returns. I'm awfully shy, you've so many people here.

OLGA. All our friends. *[Frightened, in an undertone]* You're wearing a green sash! My dear, you shouldn't!

NATASHA. Is it a sign of anything?

OLGA. No, it simply doesn't go well... and it looks so queer.

NATASHA. *[In a tearful voice]* Yes? But it isn't really green, it's too dull for that. *[Goes into dining-room with OLGA.]*

[They have all sat down to lunch in the dining-room, the sitting-room is empty.]

KULIGIN. I wish you a nice fiancée, Irina. It's quite time you married.

CHEBUTIKIN. Natalia Ivanovna, I wish you the same.

KULIGIN. Natalia Ivanovna has a fiancé already.

MASHA. *[Raps with her fork on a plate]* Let's all get drunk and make life purple for once!

KULIGIN. You've lost three good conduct marks.

VERSHININ. This is a nice drink. What's it made of?

SOLENI. Blackbeetles.

IRINA. *[Tearfully]* Phoo! How disgusting!

OLGA. There is to be a roast turkey and a sweet apple pie for dinner. Thank goodness I can spend all day and the evening at home. You'll come in the evening, ladies and gentlemen....

VERSHININ. And please may I come in the evening!

IRINA. Please do.

NATASHA. They don't stand on ceremony here.

CHEBUTIKIN. Nature only brought us into the world that we should love! *[Laughs.]*

ANDREY. *[Angrily]* Please don't! Aren't you tired of it?

[Enter FEDOTIK and RODE with a large basket of flowers.]

FEDOTIK. They're lunching already.

RODE. *[Loudly and thickly]* Lunching? Yes, so they are....

FEDOTIK. Wait a minute! *[Takes a photograph]* That's one. No, just a moment.... *[Takes another]* That's two. Now we're ready!

[They take the basket and go into the dining-room, where they have a noisy reception.]

RODE. *[Loudly]* Congratulations and best wishes! Lovely weather to-day, simply perfect. Was out walking with the High School students all the morning. I take their drills.

FEDOTIK. You may move, Irina Sergeyevna! *[Takes a photograph]* You look well to-day. *[Takes a humming-top out of his pocket]* Here's a humming-top, by the way. It's got a lovely note!

IRINA. How awfully nice!

MASHA.

> "There stands a green oak by the sea,
> And a chain of bright gold is around it...
> And a chain of bright gold is around it..."

[Tearfully] What am I saying that for? I've had those words running in my head all day....

KULIGIN. There are thirteen at table!

RODE. *[Aloud]* Surely you don't believe in that superstition? *[Laughter.]*

KULIGIN. If there are thirteen at table then it means there are lovers present. It isn't you, Ivan Romanovitch, hang it all.... *[Laughter.]*

CHEBUTIKIN. I'm a hardened sinner, but I really don't see why Natalia Ivanovna should blush....

[Loud laughter; NATASHA runs out into the sitting-room, followed by ANDREY.]

ANDREY. Don't pay any attention to them! Wait... do stop, please....

NATASHA. I'm shy... I don't know what's the matter with me and they're all laughing at me. It wasn't nice of me to leave the table like that, but I can't... I can't. *[Covers her face with her hands.]*

ANDREY. My dear, I beg you. I implore you not to excite yourself. I assure you they're only joking, they're kind people. My dear, good girl, they're all kind and sincere people, and they like both you and me. Come here to the window, they can't see us here.... *[Looks round.]*

NATASHA. I'm so unaccustomed to meeting people!

ANDREY. Oh your youth, your splendid, beautiful youth! My darling, don't be so excited! Believe me, believe me... I'm so happy, my soul is full of love, of ecstasy.... They don't see us! They can't! Why, why or when did I fall in love with you—Oh, I can't understand anything. My dear, my pure darling, be my wife! I love you, love you... as never before.... *[They kiss.]*

[Two officers come in and, seeing the lovers kiss, stop in astonishment.]

Curtain.

ACT II

[Scene as before. It is 8 p.m. Somebody is heard playing a concertina outside in' the street. There is no fire. NATALIA IVANOVNA enters in indoor dress carrying a candle; she stops by the door which leads into ANDREY'S room.]

NATASHA. What are you doing, Andrey? Are you reading? It's nothing, only I.... *[She opens another door, and looks in, then closes it]* Isn't there any fire....

ANDREY. *[Enters with book in hand]* What are you doing, Natasha?

NATASHA. I was looking to see if there wasn't a fire. It's Shrovetide, and the servant is simply beside herself; I must look out that something doesn't happen. When I came through the dining-room yesterday midnight, there was a candle burning. I couldn't get her to tell me who had lighted it. *[Puts down her candle]* What's the time?

ANDREY. *[Looks at his watch]* A quarter past eight.

NATASHA. And Olga and Irina aren't in yet. The poor things are still at work. Olga at the teacher's council, Irina at the telegraph office.... *[Sighs]* I said to your sister this morning, "Irina, darling, you must take care of yourself." But she pays no attention. Did you say it was a quarter past eight? I am afraid little Bobby is quite ill. Why is he so cold? He was feverish yesterday, but to-day he is quite cold... I am so frightened!

ANDREY. It's all right, Natasha. The boy is well.

NATASHA. Still, I think we ought to put him on a diet. I am so afraid. And the entertainers were to be here after nine; they had better not come, Audrey.

ANDREY. I don't know. After all, they were asked.

NATASHA. This morning, when the little boy woke up and saw me he suddenly smiled; that means he knew me. "Good morning, Bobby!" I said, "good morning, darling." And he laughed. Children understand, they understand very well. So I'll tell them, Andrey dear, not to receive the entertainers.

ANDREY. *[Hesitatingly]* But what about my sisters. This is their flat.

NATASHA. They'll do as I want them. They are so kind.... *[Going]* I ordered sour milk for supper. The doctor says you must eat sour milk and nothing else, or you won't get thin. *[Stops]* Bobby is so cold. I'm afraid his room is too cold for him. It would be nice to put him into another room till the warm weather comes. Irina's room, for instance, is just right for a child: it's dry and has the sun all day. I must tell her, she can share Olga's room. It isn't as if she was at home in the daytime, she only sleeps here.... *[A pause]* Andrey, darling, why are you so silent?

ANDREY. I was just thinking.... There is really nothing to say....

NATASHA. Yes... there was something I wanted to tell you.... Oh, yes. Ferapont has come from the Council offices, he wants to see you.

ANDREY. *[Yawns]* Call him here.

[NATASHA goes out; ANDREY reads his book, stooping over the candle she has left behind. FERAPONT enters; he wears a tattered old coat with the collar up. His ears are muffled.]

ANDREY. Good morning, grandfather. What have you to say?

FERAPONT. The Chairman sends a book and some documents or other. Here.... *[Hands him a book and a packet.]*

ANDREY. Thank you. It's all right. Why couldn't you come earlier? It's past eight now.

FERAPONT. What?

ANDREY. *[Louder]*. I say you've come late, it's past eight.

FERAPONT. Yes, yes. I came when it was still light, but they wouldn't let me in. They said you were busy. Well, what was I to do. If you're busy, you're busy, and I'm in no hurry. *[He thinks that ANDREY is asking him something]* What?

ANDREY. Nothing. *[Looks through the book]* To-morrow's Friday. I'm not supposed to go to work, but I'll come—all the same... and do some work. It's dull at home. *[Pause]* Oh, my dear old man, how strangely life changes, and how it deceives! To-day, out of sheer boredom, I took up this book—old university lectures, and I couldn't help laughing. My God, I'm secretary of the local district council, the council which has Protopopov for its chairman, yes, I'm the secretary, and the summit of my ambitions is—to become a member of the council! I to be a member of the local district council, I, who dream every night that I'm a professor of Moscow University, a famous scholar of whom all Russia is proud!

FERAPONT. I can't tell... I'm hard of hearing....

ANDREY. If you weren't, I don't suppose I should talk to you. I've got to talk to somebody, and my wife doesn't understand me, and I'm a bit afraid of my sisters—I don't know why unless it is that they may make fun of me and make me feel ashamed... I don't drink, I don't like public-houses, but how I should like to be sitting just now in Tyestov's place in Moscow, or at the Great Moscow, old fellow!

FERAPONT. Moscow? That's where a contractor was once telling that some merchants or other were eating pancakes; one ate forty pancakes and he went and died, he was saying. Either forty or fifty, I forget which.

ANDREY. In Moscow you can sit in an enormous restaurant where you don't know anybody and where nobody knows you, and you don't feel all the same that you're a stranger. And here you know everybody and everybody knows you, and you're a stranger... and a lonely stranger.

FERAPONT. What? And the same contractor was telling —perhaps he was lying—that there was a cable stretching right across Moscow.

ANDREY. What for?

FERAPONT. I can't tell. The contractor said so.

ANDREY. Rubbish. *[He reads]* Were you ever in Moscow?

FERAPONT. *[After a pause]* No. God did not lead me there. *[Pause]* Shall I go?

ANDREY. You may go. Good-bye. *[FERAPONT goes]* Good-bye. *[Reads]* You can come to-morrow and fetch these documents.... Go along.... *[Pause]* He's gone. *[A ring]* Yes, yes.... *[Stretches himself and slowly goes into his own room.]*

[Behind the scene the nurse is singing a lullaby to the child. MASHA and VERSHININ come in. While they talk, a maidservant lights candles and a lamp.]

MASHA. I don't know. *[Pause]* I don't know. Of course, habit counts for a great deal. After father's death, for instance, it took us a long time to get used to the absence of orderlies. But, apart from habit, it seems to me in all fairness that, however it may be in other towns, the best and most-educated people are army men.

VERSHININ. I'm thirsty. I should like some tea.

MASHA. *[Glancing at her watch]* They'll bring some soon. I was given in marriage when I was eighteen, and I was afraid of my husband because he was a teacher and I'd only just left school. He then seemed to me frightfully wise and learned and important. And now, unfortunately, that has changed.

VERSHININ. Yes... yes.

MASHA. I don't speak of my husband, I've grown used to him, but civilians in general are so often coarse, impolite, uneducated. Their rudeness offends me, it angers me. I suffer when I see that a man isn't quite sufficiently refined, or delicate, or polite. I simply suffer agonies when I happen to be among schoolmasters, my husband's colleagues.

VERSHININ. Yes.... It seems to me that civilians and army men are equally interesting, in this town, at any rate. It's all the same! If you listen to a member of the local intelligentsia, whether to civilian or military, he will tell you that he's sick of his wife, sick of his house, sick of his estate, sick of his horses.... We Russians are extremely gifted in the direction of thinking on an exalted plane, but, tell me, why do we aim so low in real life? Why?

MASHA. Why?

VERSHININ. Why is a Russian sick of his children, sick of his wife? And why are his wife and children sick of him?

MASHA. You're a little downhearted to-day.

VERSHININ. Perhaps I am. I haven't had any dinner, I've had nothing since the morning. My daughter is a little unwell, and when my girls are ill, I get very anxious and my conscience tortures me because they have such a mother. Oh, if you had seen her to-day! What a trivial personality! We began quarrelling at seven in the morning and at nine I slammed the door and went out. *[Pause]* I never speak of her, it's strange that I bear my complaints to you alone. *[Kisses her hand]* Don't be angry with me. I haven't anybody but you, nobody at all.... *[Pause.]*

MASHA. What a noise in the oven. Just before father's death there was a noise in the pipe, just like that.

VERSHININ. Are you superstitious?

MASHA. Yes.

VERSHININ. That's strange. *[Kisses her hand]* You are a splendid, wonderful woman. Splendid, wonderful! It is dark here, but I see your sparkling eyes.

MASHA. *[Sits on another chair]* There is more light here.

VERSHININ. I love you, love you, love you... I love your eyes, your movements, I dream of them.... Splendid, wonderful woman!

MASHA. *[Laughing]* When you talk to me like that, I laugh; I don't know why, for I'm afraid. Don't repeat it, please.... *[In an undertone]* No, go on, it's all the same to me.... *[Covers her face with her hands]* Somebody's coming, let's talk about something else.

[IRINA and TUZENBACH come in through the dining-room.]

TUZENBACH. My surname is really triple. I am called Baron Tuzenbach-Krone-Altschauer, but I am Russian and Orthodox, the same as you. There is very little German left in me, unless perhaps it is the patience and the obstinacy with which I bore you. I see you home every night.

IRINA. How tired I am!

TUZENBACH. And I'll come to the telegraph office to see you home every day for ten or twenty years, until you drive me away. *[He sees MASHA and VERSHININ; joyfully]* Is that you? How do you do.

IRINA. Well, I am home at last. *[To MASHA]* A lady came to-day to telegraph to her brother in Saratov that her son died to-day, and she couldn't remember the address anyhow. So she sent the telegram without an address, just to Saratov. She was crying. And for some reason or other I was rude to her. "I've no time," I said. It was so stupid. Are the entertainers coming to-night?

MASHA. Yes.

IRINA. *[Sitting down in an armchair]* I want a rest. I am tired.

TUZENBACH. *[Smiling]* When you come home from your work you seem so young, and so unfortunate.... *[Pause.]*

IRINA. I am tired. No, I don't like the telegraph office, I don't like it.

MASHA. You've grown thinner.... *[Whistles a little]* And you look younger, and your face has become like a boy's.

TUZENBACH. That's the way she does her hair.

IRINA. I must find another job, this one won't do for me. What I wanted, what I hoped to get, just that is lacking here. Labour without poetry, without ideas.... *[A knock on the floor]* The doctor is knocking. *[To TUZENBACH]* Will you knock, dear. I can't... I'm tired.... *[TUZENBACH knocks]* He'll come in a minute. Something ought to be done. Yesterday the doctor and Andrey played cards at the club and lost money. Andrey seems to have lost 200 roubles.

MASHA. *[With indifference]* What can we do now?

IRINA. He lost money a fortnight ago, he lost money in December. Perhaps if he lost everything we should go away from this town. Oh, my God, I dream of Moscow every night. I'm just like a lunatic. *[Laughs]* We go there in June, and before June there's still... February, March, April, May... nearly half a year!

MASHA. Only Natasha mustn't get to know of these losses.

IRINA. I expect it will be all the same to her.

[CHEBUTIKIN, who has only just got out of bed—he was resting after dinner—comes into the dining-room and combs his beard. He then sits by the table and takes a newspaper from his pocket.]

MASHA. Here he is.... Has he paid his rent?

IRINA. *[Laughs]* No. He's been here eight months and hasn't paid a copeck. Seems to have forgotten.

MASHA. *[Laughs]* What dignity in his pose! *[They all laugh. A pause.]*

IRINA. Why are you so silent, Alexander Ignateyevitch?

VERSHININ. I don't know. I want some tea. Half my life for a tumbler of tea: I haven't had anything since morning.

CHEBUTIKIN. Irina Sergeyevna!

IRINA. What is it?

CHEBUTIKIN. Please come here, Venez ici. *[IRINA goes and sits by the table]* I can't do without you. *[IRINA begins to play patience.]*

VERSHININ. Well, if we can't have any tea, let's philosophize, at any rate.

TUZENBACH. Yes, let's. About what?

VERSHININ. About what? Let us meditate... about life as it will be after our time; for example, in two or three hundred years.

TUZENBACH. Well? After our time people will fly about in balloons, the cut of one's coat will change, perhaps they'll discover a sixth sense and develop it, but life will remain the same, laborious, mysterious, and happy. And in a thousand years' time, people will still be sighing: "Life is hard!"—and at the same time they'll be just as afraid of death, and unwilling to meet it, as we are.

VERSHININ. [Thoughtfully] How can I put it? It seems to me that everything on earth must change, little by little, and is already changing under our very eyes. After two or three hundred years, after a thousand—the actual time doesn't matter—a new and happy age will begin. We, of course, shall not take part in it, but we live and work and even suffer to-day that it should come. We create it—and in that one object is our destiny and, if you like, our happiness.

[MASHA laughs softly.]

TUZENBACH. What is it?

MASHA. I don't know. I've been laughing all day, ever since morning.

VERSHININ. I finished my education at the same point as you, I have not studied at universities; I read a lot, but I cannot choose my books and perhaps what I read is not at all what I should, but the longer I love, the more I want to know. My hair is turning white, I am nearly an old man now, but I know so little, oh, so little! But I think I know the things that matter most, and that are most real. I know them well. And I wish I could make you understand that there is no happiness for us, that there should not and cannot be.... We must only work and work, and happiness is only for our distant posterity. *[Pause]* If not for me, then for the descendants of my descendants.

[FEDOTIK and RODE come into the dining-room; they sit and sing softly, strumming on a guitar.]

TUZENBACH. According to you, one should not even think about happiness! But suppose I am happy!

VERSHININ. No.

TUZENBACH. *[Moves his hands and laughs]* We do not seem to understand each other. How can I convince you? *[MASHA laughs quietly, TUZENBACH continues, pointing at her]* Yes, laugh! *[To VERSHININ]* Not only after two or three centuries, but in a million years, life will still be as it was; life does not change, it remains for ever, following its own laws which do not concern us, or which, at any rate, you will never find out. Migrant birds, cranes for example, fly and fly, and whatever thoughts, high or low, enter their heads, they will still fly and not know why or where. They fly and will continue to fly, whatever philosophers come to life among them; they may philosophize as much as they like, only they will fly....

MASHA. Still, is there a meaning?

TUZENBACH. A meaning.... Now the snow is falling. What meaning? *[Pause.]*

MASHA. It seems to me that a man must have faith, or must search for a faith, or his life will be empty, empty....

To live and not to know why the cranes fly, why babies are born, why there are stars in the sky.... Either you must know why you live, or everything is trivial, not worth a straw. *[A pause.]*

VERSHININ. Still, I am sorry that my youth has gone.

MASHA. Gogol says: life in this world is a dull matter, my masters!

TUZENBACH. And I say it's difficult to argue with you, my masters! Hang it all.

CHEBUTIKIN. *[Reading]* Balzac was married at Berdichev. *[IRINA is singing softly]* That's worth making a note of. *[He makes a note]* Balzac was married at Berdichev. *[Goes on reading.]*

IRINA. *[Laying out cards, thoughtfully]* Balzac was married at Berdichev.

TUZENBACH. The die is cast. I've handed in my resignation, Maria Sergeyevna.

MASHA. So I heard. I don't see what good it is; I don't like civilians.

TUZENBACH. Never mind.... *[Gets up]* I'm not handsome; what use am I as a soldier? Well, it makes no difference... I shall work. If only just once in my life I could work so that I could come home in the evening, fall exhausted on my bed, and go to sleep at once. *[Going into the dining-room]* Workmen, I suppose, do sleep soundly!

FEDOTIK. *[To IRINA]* I bought some coloured pencils for you at Pizhikov's in the Moscow Road, just now. And here is a little knife.

IRINA. You have got into the habit of behaving to me as if I am a little girl, but I am grown up. *[Takes the pencils and the knife, then, with joy]* How lovely!

FEDOTIK. And I bought myself a knife... look at it... one blade, another, a third, an ear-scoop, scissors, nail-cleaners.

RODE. *[Loudly]* Doctor, how old are you?

CHEBUTIKIN. I? Thirty-two. *[Laughter]*

FEDOTIK. I'll show you another kind of patience.... *[Lays out cards.]*

[A samovar is brought in; ANFISA attends to it; a little later NATASHA enters and helps by the table; SOLENI arrives and, after greetings, sits by the table.]

VERSHININ. What a wind!

MASHA. Yes. I'm tired of winter. I've already forgotten what summer's like.

IRINA. It's coming out, I see. We're going to Moscow.

FEDOTIK. No, it won't come out. Look, the eight was on the two of spades. *[Laughs]* That means you won't go to Moscow.

CHEBUTIKIN. *[Reading paper]* Tsitsigar. Smallpox is raging here.

ANFISA. *[Coming up to MASHA]* Masha, have some tea, little mother. *[To VERSHININ]* Please have some, sir... excuse me, but I've forgotten your name....

MASHA. Bring some here, nurse. I shan't go over there.

IRINA. Nurse!

ANFISA. Coming, coming!

NATASHA. *[To SOLENI]* Children at the breast understand perfectly. I said "Good morning, Bobby; good morning, dear!" And he looked at me in quite an unusual way. You think it's only the mother in me that is speaking; I assure you that isn't so! He's a wonderful child.

SOLENI. If he was my child I'd roast him on a frying-pan and eat him. *[Takes his tumbler into the drawing-room and sits in a corner.]*

NATASHA. *[Covers her face in her hands]* Vulgar, ill-bred man!

MASHA. He's lucky who doesn't notice whether it's winter now, or summer. I think that if I were in Moscow, I shouldn't mind about the weather.

VERSHININ. A few days ago I was reading the prison diary of a French minister. He had been sentenced on account of the Panama scandal. With what joy, what delight, he speaks of the birds he saw through the prison windows, which he had never noticed while he was a minister. Now, of course, that he is at liberty, he notices birds no more than he did before. When you go to live in

Moscow you'll not notice it, in just the same way. There
can be no happiness for us, it only exists in our wishes.

TUZENBACH. *[Takes cardboard box from the table]* Where
are the pastries?

IRINA. Soleni has eaten them.

TUZENBACH. All of them?

ANFISA. *[Serving tea]* There's a letter for you.

VERSHININ. For me? *[Takes the letter]* From my daughter.
[Reads] Yes, of course... I will go quietly. Excuse me,
Maria Sergeyevna. I shan't have any tea. *[Stands up, excited]*
That eternal story....

MASHA. What is it? Is it a secret?

VERSHININ. *[Quietly]* My wife has poisoned herself
again. I must go. I'll go out quietly. It's all awfully
unpleasant. *[Kisses MASHA'S hand]* My dear, my splendid,
good woman... I'll go this way, quietly. *[Exit.]*

ANFISA. Where has he gone? And I'd served tea.... What
a man.

MASHA. *[Angrily]* Be quiet! You bother so one can't have
a moment's peace.... *[Goes to the table with her cup]* I'm tired
of you, old woman!

ANFISA. My dear! Why are you offended!

ANDREY'S VOICE. Anfisa!

ANFISA. *[Mocking]* Anfisa! He sits there and... *[Exit.]*

MASHA. *[In the dining-room, by the table angrily]* Let me sit down! *[Disturbs the cards on the table]* Here you are, spreading your cards out. Have some tea!

IRINA. You are cross, Masha.

MASHA. If I am cross, then don't talk to me. Don't touch me!

CHEBUTIKIN. Don't touch her, don't touch her....

MASHA. You're sixty, but you're like a boy, always up to some beastly nonsense.

NATASHA. *[Sighs]* Dear Masha, why use such expressions? With your beautiful exterior you would be simply fascinating in good society, I tell you so directly, if it wasn't for your words. *Je vous prie, pardonnez moi, Marie, mais vous avez des manières un peu grossières.*

TUZENBACH. *[Restraining his laughter]* Give me... give me... there's some cognac, I think.

NATASHA. *Il paraît, que mon Bobick déjà ne dort pas,* he has awakened. He isn't well to-day. I'll go to him, excuse me... *[Exit.]*

IRINA. Where has Alexander Ignateyevitch gone?

MASHA. Home. Something extraordinary has happened to his wife again.

TUZENBACH. *[Goes to SOLENI with a cognac-flask in his hands]* You go on sitting by yourself, thinking of something —goodness knows what. Come and let's make peace.

Let's have some cognac. *[They drink]* I expect I'll have to play the piano all night, some rubbish most likely... well, so be it!

SOLENI. Why make peace? I haven't quarrelled with you.

TUZENBACH. You always make me feel as if something has taken place between us. You've a strange character, you must admit.

SOLENI. *[Declaims]* "I am strange, but who is not? Don't be angry, Aleko!"

TUZENBACH. And what has Aleko to do with it? *[Pause.]*

SOLENI. When I'm with one other man I behave just like everybody else, but in company I'm dull and shy and... talk all manner of rubbish. But I'm more honest and more honourable than very, very many people. And I can prove it.

TUZENBACH. I often get angry with you, you always fasten on to me in company, but I like you all the same. I'm going to drink my fill to-night, whatever happens. Drink, now!

SOLENI. Let's drink. *[They drink]* I never had anything against you, Baron. But my character is like Lermontov's *[In a low voice]* I even rather resemble Lermontov, they say.... *[Takes a scent-bottle from his pocket, and scents his hands.]*

TUZENBACH. I've sent in my resignation. Basta! I've been thinking about it for five years, and at last made up my mind. I shall work.

SOLENI. *[Declaims]* "Do not be angry, Aleko... forget, forget, thy dreams of yore...."

[While he is speaking ANDREY enters quietly with a book, and sits by the table.]

TUZENBACH. I shall work.

CHEBUTIKIN. *[Going with IRINA into the dining-room]* And the food was also real Caucasian onion soup, and, for a roast, some chehartma.

SOLENI. Cheremsha *[Note: A variety of garlic.]* isn't meat at all, but a plant something like an onion.

CHEBUTIKIN. No, my angel. Chehartma isn't onion, but roast mutton.

SOLENI. And I tell you, chehartma—is a sort of onion.

CHEBUTIKIN. And I tell you, chehartma—is mutton.

SOLENI. And I tell you, cheremsha—is a sort of onion.

CHEBUTIKIN. What's the use of arguing! You've never been in the Caucasus, and never ate any chehartma.

SOLENI. I never ate it, because I hate it. It smells like garlic.

ANDREY. *[Imploring]* Please, please! I ask you!

TUZENBACH. When are the entertainers coming?

IRINA. They promised for about nine; that is, quite soon.

TUZENBACH. *[Embraces ANDREY]*

> "Oh my house, my house, my new-built
>   house."

ANDREY. *[Dances and sings]* "Newly-built of maple-wood."

CHEBUTIKIN. *[Dances]*

> "Its walls are like a sieve!" *[Laughter.]*

TUZENBACH. *[Kisses ANDREY]* Hang it all, let's drink. Andrey, old boy, let's drink with you. And I'll go with you, Andrey, to the University of Moscow.

SOLENI. Which one? There are two universities in Moscow.

ANDREY. There's one university in Moscow.

SOLENI. Two, I tell you.

ANDREY. Don't care if there are three. So much the better.

SOLENI. There are two universities in Moscow! *[There are murmurs and "hushes"]* There are two universities in Moscow, the old one and the new one. And if you don't like to listen, if my words annoy you, then I need not speak. I can even go into another room.... *[Exit.]*

TUZENBACH. Bravo, bravo! *[Laughs]* Come on, now. I'm going to play. Funny man, Soleni.... *[Goes to the piano and plays a waltz.]*

MASHA. *[Dancing solo]* The Baron's drunk, the Baron's drunk, the Baron's drunk!

[NATASHA comes in.]

NATASHA. *[To CHEBUTIKIN]* Ivan Romanovitch!

[Says something to CHEBUTIKIN, then goes out quietly; CHEBUTIKIN touches TUZENBACH on the shoulder and whispers something to him.]

IRINA. What is it?

CHEBUTIKIN. Time for us to go. Good-bye.

TUZENBACH. Good-night. It's time we went.

IRINA. But, really, the entertainers?

ANDREY. *[In confusion]* There won't be any entertainers. You see, dear, Natasha says that Bobby isn't quite well, and so.... In a word, I don't care, and it's absolutely all one to me.

IRINA. *[Shrugging her shoulders]* Bobby ill!

MASHA. What is she thinking of! Well, if they are sent home, I suppose they must go. *[To IRINA]* Bobby's all right, it's she herself.... Here! *[Taps her forehead]* Little bourgeoise!

[ANDREY goes to his room through the right-hand door, CHEBUTIKIN follows him. In the dining-room they are saying good-bye.]

FEDOTIK. What a shame! I was expecting to spend the evening here, but of course, if the little baby is ill... I'll bring him some toys to-morrow.

RODE. *[Loudly]* I slept late after dinner to-day because I thought I was going to dance all night. It's only nine o'clock now!

MASHA. Let's go into the street, we can talk there. Then we can settle things.

(Good-byes and good nights are heard. TUZENBACH'S merry laughter is heard. *[All go out]* ANFISA and the maid clear the table, and put out the lights. *[The nurse sings]* ANDREY, wearing an overcoat and a hat, and CHEBUTIKIN enter silently.)

CHEBUTIKIN. I never managed to get married because my life flashed by like lightning, and because I was madly in love with your mother, who was married.

ANDREY. One shouldn't marry. One shouldn't, because it's dull.

CHEBUTIKIN. So there I am, in my loneliness. Say what you will, loneliness is a terrible thing, old fellow.... Though really... of course, it absolutely doesn't matter!

ANDREY. Let's be quicker.

CHEBUTIKIN. What are you in such a hurry for? We shall be in time.

ANDREY. I'm afraid my wife may stop me.

CHEBUTIKIN. Ah!

ANDREY. I shan't play to-night, I shall only sit and look on. I don't feel very well.... What am I to do for my asthma, Ivan Romanovitch?

CHEBUTIKIN. Don't ask me! I don't remember, old fellow, I don't know.

ANDREY. Let's go through the kitchen. *[They go out.]*

[A bell rings, then a second time; voices and laughter are heard.]

IRINA. *[Enters]* What's that?

ANFISA. *[Whispers]* The entertainers! *[Bell.]*

IRINA. Tell them there's nobody at home, nurse. They must excuse us.

[ANFISA goes out. IRINA walks about the room deep in thought; she is excited. SOLENI enters.]

SOLENI. *[In surprise]* There's nobody here.... Where are they all?

IRINA. They've gone home.

SOLENI. How strange. Are you here alone?

IRINA. Yes, alone. *[A pause]* Good-bye.

SOLENI. Just now I behaved tactlessly, with insufficient reserve. But you are not like all the others, you are noble and pure, you can see the truth.... You alone can understand me. I love you, deeply, beyond measure, I love you.

IRINA. Good-bye! Go away.

SOLENI. I cannot live without you. *[Follows her]* Oh, my happiness! *[Through his tears]* Oh, joy! Wonderful, marvellous, glorious eyes, such as I have never seen before....

IRINA. *[Coldly]* Stop it, Vassili Vassilevitch!

SOLENI. This is the first time I speak to you of love, and it is as if I am no longer on the earth, but on another planet. *[Wipes his forehead]* Well, never mind. I can't make you love me by force, of course... but I don't intend to have any more-favoured rivals.... No... I swear to you by all the saints, I shall kill my rival.... Oh, beautiful one!

[NATASHA enters with a candle; she looks in through one door, then through another, and goes past the door leading to her husband's room.]

NATASHA. Here's Andrey. Let him go on reading. Excuse me, Vassili Vassilevitch, I did not know you were here; I am engaged in domesticities.

SOLENI. It's all the same to me. Good-bye! *[Exit.]*

NATASHA. You're so tired, my poor dear girl! *[Kisses IRINA]* If you only went to bed earlier.

IRINA. Is Bobby asleep?

NATASHA. Yes, but restlessly. By the way, dear, I wanted to tell you, but either you weren't at home, or I was busy... I think Bobby's present nursery is cold and damp. And your room would be so nice for the child. My dear, darling girl, do change over to Olga's for a bit!

IRINA. [*Not understanding*] Where?

[*The bells of a troika are heard as it drives up to the house.*]

NATASHA. You and Olga can share a room, for the time being, and Bobby can have yours. He's such a darling; to-day I said to him, "Bobby, you're mine! Mine!" And he looked at me with his dear little eyes. [*A bell rings*] It must be Olga. How late she is! [*The maid enters and whispers to NATASHA*] Protopopov? What a queer man to do such a thing. Protopopov's come and wants me to go for a drive with him in his troika. [*Laughs*] How funny these men are.... [*A bell rings*] Somebody has come. Suppose I did go and have half an hour's drive.... [*To the maid*] Say I shan't be long. [*Bell rings*] Somebody's ringing, it must be Olga. [*Exit.*]

[*The maid runs out; IRINA sits deep in thought; KULIGIN and OLGA enter, followed by VERSHININ.*]

KULIGIN. Well, there you are. And you said there was going to be a party.

VERSHININ. It's queer; I went away not long ago, half an hour ago, and they were expecting entertainers.

IRINA. They've all gone.

KULIGIN. Has Masha gone too? Where has she gone? And what's Protopopov waiting for downstairs in his troika? Whom is he expecting?

IRINA. Don't ask questions... I'm tired.

KULIGIN. Oh, you're all whimsies....

OLGA. My committee meeting is only just over. I'm tired out. Our chairwoman is ill, so I had to take her place. My head, my head is aching.... *[Sits]* Andrey lost 200 roubles at cards yesterday... the whole town is talking about it....

KULIGIN. Yes, my meeting tired me too. *[Sits.]*

VERSHININ. My wife took it into her head to frighten me just now by nearly poisoning herself. It's all right now, and I'm glad; I can rest now.... But perhaps we ought to go away? Well, my best wishes, Feodor Ilitch, let's go somewhere together! I can't, I absolutely can't stop at home.... Come on!

KULIGIN. I'm tired. I won't go. *[Gets up]* I'm tired. Has my wife gone home?

IRINA. I suppose so.

KULIGIN. *[Kisses IRINA'S hand]* Good-bye, I'm going to rest all day to-morrow and the day after. Best wishes! *[Going]* I should like some tea. I was looking forward to spending the whole evening in pleasant company and—o, fallacem hominum spem!... Accusative case after an interjection....

VERSHININ. Then I'll go somewhere by myself. *[Exit with KULIGIN, whistling.]*

OLGA. I've such a headache... Andrey has been losing money.... The whole town is talking.... I'll go and lie down. *[Going]* I'm free to-morrow.... Oh, my God, what a mercy! I'm free to-morrow, I'm free the day after.... Oh my head, my head.... *[Exit.]*

IRINA. *[alone]* They've all gone. Nobody's left.

[A concertina is being played in the street. The nurse sings.]

NATASHA. *[in fur coat and cap, steps across the dining-room, followed by the maid]* I'll be back in half an hour. I'm only going for a little drive. *[Exit.]*

IRINA. *[Alone in her misery]* To Moscow! Moscow! Moscow!

Curtain.

ACT III

[The room shared by OLGA and IRINA. Beds, screened off, on the right and left. It is past 2 a.m. Behind the stage a fire-alarm is ringing; it has apparently been going for some time. Nobody in the house has gone to bed yet. MASHA is lying on a sofa dressed, as usual, in black. Enter OLGA and ANFISA.]

ANFISA. Now they are downstairs, sitting under the stairs. I said to them, "Won't you come up," I said, "You can't go on like this," and they simply cried, "We don't know where father is." They said, "He may be burnt up by now." What an idea! And in the yard there are some people... also undressed.

OLGA. *[Takes a dress out of the cupboard]* Take this grey dress.... And this... and the blouse as well.... Take the skirt, too, nurse.... My God! How awful it is! The whole of the Kirsanovsky Road seems to have burned down. Take this... and this.... *[Throws clothes into her hands]* The poor Vershinins are so frightened.... Their house was nearly burnt. They ought to come here for the night.... They shouldn't be allowed to go home.... Poor Fedotik is completely burnt out, there's nothing left....

ANFISA. Couldn't you call Ferapont, Olga dear. I can hardly manage....

OLGA. *[Rings]* They'll never answer.... *[At the door]* Come here, whoever there is! *[Through the open door can be seen a window, red with flame: afire-engine is heard passing the house]* How awful this is. And how I'm sick of it! *[FERAPONT enters]* Take these things down.... The Kolotilin girls are down below... and let them have them. This, too.

FERAPONT. Yes'm. In the year twelve Moscow was burning too. Oh, my God! The Frenchmen were surprised.

OLGA. Go on, go on....

FERAPONT. Yes'm. *[Exit.]*

OLGA. Nurse, dear, let them have everything. We don't want anything. Give it all to them, nurse.... I'm tired, I can hardly keep on my legs.... The Vershinins mustn't be allowed to go home.... The girls can sleep in the drawing-room, and Alexander Ignateyevitch can go downstairs to the Baron's flat... Fedotik can go there, too, or else into our dining-room.... The doctor is drunk, beastly drunk, as if on purpose, so nobody can go to him. Vershinin's wife, too, may go into the drawing-room.

ANFISA. *[Tired]* Olga, dear girl, don't dismiss me! Don't dismiss me!

OLGA. You're talking nonsense, nurse. Nobody is dismissing you.

ANFISA. *[Puts OLGA'S head against her bosom]* My dear, precious girl, I'm working, I'm toiling away... I'm growing weak, and they'll all say go away! And where shall I go? Where? I'm eighty. Eighty-one years old....

OLGA. You sit down, nurse dear.... You're tired, poor dear.... *[Makes her sit down]* Rest, dear. You're so pale!

[NATASHA comes in.]

NATASHA. They are saying that a committee to assist the sufferers from the fire must be formed at once. What do you think of that? It's a beautiful idea. Of course the poor ought to be helped, it's the duty of the rich. Bobby and little Sophy are sleeping, sleeping as if nothing at all was the matter. There's such a lot of people here, the place is full of them, wherever you go. There's influenza in the town now. I'm afraid the children may catch it.

OLGA. *[Not attending]* In this room we can't see the fire, it's quiet here.

NATASHA. Yes... I suppose I'm all untidy. *[Before the looking-glass]* They say I'm growing stout... it isn't true! Certainly it isn't! Masha's asleep; the poor thing is tired out.... *[Coldly, to ANFISA]* Don't dare to be seated in my presence! Get up! Out of this! *[Exit ANFISA; a pause]* I don't understand what makes you keep on that old woman!

OLGA. *[Confusedly]* Excuse me, I don't understand either...

NATASHA. She's no good here. She comes from the country, she ought to live there.... Spoiling her, I call it! I like order in the house! We don't want any unnecessary people here. *[Strokes her cheek]* You're tired, poor thing! Our head mistress is tired! And when my little Sophie grows up and goes to school I shall be so afraid of you.

OLGA. I shan't be head mistress.

NATASHA. They'll appoint you, Olga. It's settled.

OLGA. I'll refuse the post. I can't... I'm not strong enough.... *[Drinks water]* You were so rude to nurse just now... I'm sorry. I can't stand it... everything seems dark in front of me....

NATASHA. *[Excited]* Forgive me, Olga, forgive me... I didn't want to annoy you.

[MASHA gets up, takes a pillow and goes out angrily.]

OLGA. Remember, dear... we have been brought up, in an unusual way, perhaps, but I can't bear this. Such behaviour has a bad effect on me, I get ill... I simply lose heart!

NATASHA. Forgive me, forgive me.... *[Kisses her.]*

OLGA. Even the least bit of rudeness, the slightest impoliteness, upsets me.

NATASHA. I often say too much, it's true, but you must agree, dear, that she could just as well live in the country.

OLGA. She has been with us for thirty years.

NATASHA. But she can't do any work now. Either I don't understand, or you don't want to understand me. She's no good for work, she can only sleep or sit about.

OLGA. And let her sit about.

NATASHA. *[Surprised]* What do you mean? She's only a servant. *[Crying]* I don't understand you, Olga. I've got a nurse, a wet-nurse, we've a cook, a housemaid... what do we want that old woman for as well? What good is she? *[Fire-alarm behind the stage.]*

OLGA. I've grown ten years older to-night.

NATASHA. We must come to an agreement, Olga. Your place is the school, mine——the home. You devote yourself to teaching, I, to the household. And if I talk about servants, then I do know what I am talking about; I do know what I am talking about... And to-morrow there's to be no more of that old thief, that old hag... *[Stamping]* that witch! And don't you dare to annoy me! Don't you dare! *[Stopping short]* Really, if you don't move downstairs, we shall always be quarrelling. This is awful.

[Enter KULIGIN.]

KULIGIN. Where's Masha? It's time we went home. The fire seems to be going down. *[Stretches himself]* Only one block has burnt down, but there was such a wind that it seemed at first the whole town was going to burn. *[Sits]* I'm tired out. My dear Olga... I often think that if it hadn't been for Masha, I should have married you. You are awfully nice.... I am absolutely tired out. *[Listens.]*

OLGA. What is it?

KULIGIN. The doctor, of course, has been drinking hard; he's terribly drunk. He might have done it on purpose! *[Gets up]* He seems to be coming here.... Do you hear him? Yes, here.... *[Laughs]* What a man... really... I'll hide myself. *[Goes to the cupboard and stands in the corner]* What a rogue.

OLGA. He hadn't touched a drop for two years, and now he suddenly goes and gets drunk....

[Retires with NATASHA to the back of the room. CHEBUTIKIN enters; apparently sober, he stops, looks round, then goes to the washstand and begins to wash his hands.]

CHEBUTIKIN. *[Angrily]* Devil take them all... take them all.... They think I'm a doctor and can cure everything, and I know absolutely nothing, I've forgotten all I ever knew, I remember nothing, absolutely nothing. *[OLGA and NATASHA go out, unnoticed by him]* Devil take it. Last Wednesday I attended a woman in Zasip—and she died, and it's my fault that she died. Yes... I used to know a certain amount five-and-twenty years ago, but I don't remember anything now. Nothing. Perhaps I'm not really a man, and am only pretending that I've got arms and legs and a head; perhaps I don't exist at all, and only imagine that I walk, and eat, and sleep. *[Cries]* Oh, if only I didn't exist! *[Stops crying; angrily]* The devil only knows.... Day before yesterday they were talking in the club; they said, Shakespeare, Voltaire... I'd never read, never read at all, and I put on an expression as if I had read. And so did the others. Oh, how beastly! How petty! And then I remembered the woman I killed on Wednesday... and I couldn't get her out of my mind, and everything in my mind became crooked, nasty, wretched.... So I went and drank....

[IRINA, VERSHININ and TUZENBACH enter; TUZENBACH is wearing new and fashionable civilian clothes.]

IRINA. Let's sit down here. Nobody will come in here.

VERSHININ. The whole town would have been destroyed if it hadn't been for the soldiers. Good men! *[Rubs his hands appreciatively]* Splendid people! Oh, what a fine lot!

KULIGIN. *[Coming up to him]* What's the time?

TUZENBACH. It's past three now. It's dawning.

IRINA. They are all sitting in the dining-room, nobody is going. And that Soleni of yours is sitting there. *[To CHEBUTIKIN]* Hadn't you better be going to sleep, doctor?

CHEBUTIKIN. It's all right... thank you.... *[Combs his beard.]*

KULIGIN. *[Laughs]* Speaking's a bit difficult, eh, Ivan Romanovitch! *[Pats him on the shoulder]* Good man! *In vino veritas*, the ancients used to say.

TUZENBACH. They keep on asking me to get up a concert in aid of the sufferers.

IRINA. As if one could do anything....

TUZENBACH. It might be arranged, if necessary. In my opinion Maria Sergeyevna is an excellent pianist.

KULIGIN. Yes, excellent!

IRINA. She's forgotten everything. She hasn't played for three years... or four.

TUZENBACH. In this town absolutely nobody understands music, not a soul except myself, but I do understand it, and assure you on my word of honour that Maria Sergeyevna plays excellently, almost with genius.

KULIGIN. You are right, Baron, I'm awfully fond of Masha. She's very fine.

TUZENBACH. To be able to play so admirably and to realize at the same time that nobody, nobody can understand you!

KULIGIN. *[Sighs]* Yes.... But will it be quite all right for her to take part in a concert? *[Pause]* You see, I don't know anything about it. Perhaps it will even be all to the good. Although I must admit that our Director is a good man, a very good man even, a very clever man, still he has such views.... Of course it isn't his business but still, if you wish it, perhaps I'd better talk to him.

[CHEBUTIKIN takes a porcelain clock into his hands and examines it.]

VERSHININ. I got so dirty while the fire was on, I don't look like anybody on earth. *[Pause]* Yesterday I happened to hear, casually, that they want to transfer our brigade to some distant place. Some said to Poland, others, to Chita.

TUZENBACH. I heard so, too. Well, if it is so, the town will be quite empty.

IRINA. And we'll go away, too!

CHEBUTIKIN. *[Drops the clock which breaks to pieces]* To smithereens!

[A pause; everybody is pained and confused.]

KULIGIN. *[Gathering up the pieces]* To smash such a valuable object—oh, Ivan Romanovitch, Ivan Romanovitch! A very bad mark for your misbehaviour!

IRINA. That clock used to belong to our mother.

CHEBUTIKIN. Perhaps.... To your mother, your mother. Perhaps I didn't break it; it only looks as if I broke it. Perhaps we only think that we exist, when really we don't. I don't know anything, nobody knows anything. *[At the door]* What are you looking at? Natasha has a little romance with Protopopov, and you don't see it.... There you sit and see nothing, and Natasha has a little romance with Protopovov.... *[Sings]* Won't you please accept this date.... *[Exit.]*

VERSHININ. Yes. *[Laughs]* How strange everything really is! *[Pause]* When the fire broke out, I hurried off home; when I get there I see the house is whole, uninjured, and in no danger, but my two girls are standing by the door in just their underclothes, their mother isn't there, the crowd is excited, horses and dogs are running about, and the girls' faces are so agitated, terrified, beseeching, and I don't know what else. My heart was pained when I saw those faces. My God, I thought, what these girls will have to put up with if they live long! I caught them up and ran, and still kept on thinking the one thing: what they will have to live through in this world! *[Fire-alarm; a pause]* I come here and find their mother shouting and angry. *[MASHA enters with a pillow and sits on the sofa]* And when my girls were standing by the door in just their underclothes, and the street was red from the fire, there was a dreadful noise, and I thought that something of the sort used to happen many years ago when an enemy made a sudden attack, and looted, and burned.... And at the same time what a difference there really is between the present and the past! And when a little more time has gone by, in two or three hundred years perhaps, people will look at our present life with just the same fear, and the same contempt, and the whole past will seem clumsy and dull, and very uncomfortable, and strange. Oh, indeed, what a life there will be, what a life! *[Laughs]* Forgive me, I've dropped into philosophy again. Please let me continue. I do awfully want to philosophize, it's just how I feel at present. *[Pause]* As if they are all asleep. As I was saying: what a life there will be! Only just imagine.... There are only three persons like yourselves in the town just now, but in future generations there will be more and more, and still more, and the time will come when everything will change and become as you would have it, people will live as you do, and then you too will go out of date; people will be born who are better than you.... *[Laughs]* Yes, to-day I am quite exceptionally in the vein. I am devilishly keen on living.... *[Sings.]*

"The power of love all ages know,
    From its assaults great good does grow."
    [Laughs.]

MASHA. Trum-tum-tum...

VERSHININ. Tum-tum...

MASHA. Tra-ra-ra?

VERSHININ. Tra-ta-ta. *[Laughs.]*

[Enter FEDOTIK.]

FEDOTIK. *[Dancing]* I'm burnt out, I'm burnt out! Down to the ground! *[Laughter.]*

IRINA. I don't see anything funny about it. Is everything burnt?

FEDOTIK. *[Laughs]* Absolutely. Nothing left at all. The guitar's burnt, and the photographs are burnt, and all my

correspondence.... And I was going to make you a present
of a note-book, and that's burnt too.

[SOLENI comes in.]

IRINA. No, you can't come here, Vassili Vassilevitch.
Please go away.

SOLENI. Why can the Baron come here and I can't?

VERSHININ. We really must go. How's the fire?

SOLENI. They say it's going down. No, I absolutely don't
see why the Baron can, and I can't? *[Scents his hands.]*

VERSHININ. Trum-tum-tum.

MASHA. Trum-tum.

VERSHININ. *[Laughs to SOLENI]* Let's go into the
dining-room.

SOLENI. Very well, we'll make a note of it. "If I should
try to make this clear, the geese would be annoyed, I
fear." *[Looks at TUZENBACH]* There, there, there.... *[Goes
out with VERSHININ and FEDOTIK.]*

IRINA. How Soleni smelt of tobacco.... *[In surprise]* The
Baron's asleep! Baron! Baron!

TUZENBACH. *[Waking]* I am tired, I must say.... The
brickworks.... No, I'm not wandering, I mean it; I'm going
to start work soon at the brickworks... I've already talked
it over. *[Tenderly, to IRINA]* You're so pale, and beautiful,
and charming.... Your paleness seems to shine through the

dark air as if it was a light.... You are sad, displeased with life.... Oh, come with me, let's go and work together!

MASHA. Nicolai Lvovitch, go away from here.

TUZENBACH. *[Laughs]* Are you here? I didn't see you. *[Kisses IRINA'S hand]* good-bye, I'll go... I look at you now and I remember, as if it was long ago, your name-day, when you, cheerfully and merrily, were talking about the joys of labour.... And how happy life seemed to me, then! What has happened to it now? *[Kisses her hand]* There are tears in your eyes. Go to bed now; it is already day... the morning begins.... If only I was allowed to give my life for you!

MASHA. Nicolai Lvovitch, go away! What business...

TUZENBACH. I'm off. *[Exit.]*

MASHA. *[Lies down]* Are you asleep, Feodor?

KULIGIN. Eh?

MASHA. Shouldn't you go home.

KULIGIN. My dear Masha, my darling Masha....

IRINA. She's tired out. You might let her rest, Fedia.

KULIGIN. I'll go at once. My wife's a good, splendid... I love you, my only one....

MASHA. *[Angrily]* Amo, amas, amat, amamus, amatis, amant.

KULIGIN. *[Laughs]* No, she really is wonderful. I've been your husband seven years, and it seems as if I was only married yesterday. On my word. No, you really are a wonderful woman. I'm satisfied, I'm satisfied, I'm satisfied!

MASHA. I'm bored, I'm bored, I'm bored.... *[Sits up]* But I can't get it out of my head.... It's simply disgraceful. It has been gnawing away at me... I can't keep silent. I mean about Andrey.... He has mortgaged this house with the bank, and his wife has got all the money; but the house doesn't belong to him alone, but to the four of us! He ought to know that, if he's an honourable man.

KULIGIN. What's the use, Masha? Andrey is in debt all round; well, let him do as he pleases.

MASHA. It's disgraceful, anyway. *[Lies down]*

KULIGIN. You and I are not poor. I work, take my classes, give private lessons... I am a plain, honest man... *Omnia mea mecum porto*, as they say.

MASHA. I don't want anything, but the unfairness of it disgusts me. *[Pause]* You go, Feodor.

KULIGIN. *[Kisses her]* You're tired, just rest for half an hour, and I'll sit and wait for you. Sleep.... *[Going]* I'm satisfied, I'm satisfied, I'm satisfied. *[Exit.]*

IRINA. Yes, really, our Andrey has grown smaller; how he's snuffed out and aged with that woman! He used to want to be a professor, and yesterday he was boasting that at last he had been made a member of the district council. He is a member, and Protopopov is chairman.... The whole town talks and laughs about it, and he alone knows and sees nothing.... And now everybody's gone to look at the fire, but he sits alone in his room and pays no attention, only just plays on his fiddle. *[Nervily]* Oh, it's awful, awful, awful. *[Weeps]* I can't, I can't bear it any longer!... I can't, I can't!... *[OLGA comes in and clears up at her little table. IRINA is sobbing loudly]* Throw me out, throw me out, I can't bear any more!

OLGA. *[Alarmed]* What is it, what is it? Dear!

IRINA. *[Sobbing]* Where? Where has everything gone? Where is it all? Oh my God, my God! I've forgotten everything, everything... I don't remember what is the Italian for window or, well, for ceiling... I forget everything, every day I forget it, and life passes and will never return, and we'll never go away to Moscow... I see that we'll never go....

OLGA. Dear, dear....

IRINA. *[Controlling herself]* Oh, I am unhappy... I can't work, I shan't work. Enough, enough! I used to be a telegraphist, now I work at the town council offices, and I have nothing but hate and contempt for all they give me to do... I am already twenty-three, I have already been at work for a long while, and my brain has dried up, and I've grown thinner, plainer, older, and there is no relief of any sort, and time goes and it seems all the while as if I am going away from the real, the beautiful life, farther and farther away, down some precipice. I'm in despair and I can't understand how it is that I am still alive, that I haven't killed myself.

OLGA. Don't cry, dear girl, don't cry... I suffer, too.

IRINA. I'm not crying, not crying.... Enough.... Look, I'm not crying any more. Enough... enough!

OLGA. Dear, I tell you as a sister and a friend if you want my advice, marry the Baron. *[IRINA cries softly]* You respect him, you think highly of him.... It is true that he is not handsome, but he is so honourable and clean... people don't marry from love, but in order to do one's duty. I think so, at any rate, and I'd marry without being in love. Whoever he was, I should marry him, so long as he was a decent man. Even if he was old....

IRINA. I was always waiting until we should be settled in Moscow, there I should meet my true love; I used to think about him, and love him.... But it's all turned out to be nonsense, all nonsense....

OLGA. *[Embraces her sister]* My dear, beautiful sister, I understand everything; when Baron Nicolai Lvovitch left the army and came to us in evening dress, *[Note: I.e. in the correct dress for making a proposal of marriage.]* he seemed so bad-looking to me that I even started crying.... He asked, "What are you crying for?" How could I tell him! But if God brought him to marry you, I should be happy. That would be different, quite different.

[NATASHA with a candle walks across the stage from right to left without saying anything.]

MASHA. *[Sitting up]* She walks as if she's set something on fire.

OLGA. Masha, you're silly, you're the silliest of the family. Please forgive me for saying so. *[Pause.]*

MASHA. I want to make a confession, dear sisters. My soul is in pain. I will confess to you, and never again to anybody... I'll tell you this minute. *[Softly]* It's my secret but you must know everything... I can't be silent.... *[Pause]* I love, I love... I love that man.... You saw him only just now.... Why don't I say it... in one word. I love Vershinin.

OLGA. *[Goes behind her screen]* Stop that, I don't hear you in any case.

MASHA. What am I to do? *[Takes her head in her hands]* First he seemed queer to me, then I was sorry for him... then I fell in love with him... fell in love with his voice, his words, his misfortunes, his two daughters.

OLGA. *[Behind the screen]* I'm not listening. You may talk any nonsense you like, it will be all the same, I shan't hear.

MASHA. Oh, Olga, you are foolish. I am in love—that means that is to be my fate. It means that is to be my lot.... And he loves me.... It is all awful. Yes; it isn't good, is it? *[Takes IRINA'S hand and draws her to her]* Oh, my dear.... How are we going to live through our lives, what is to become of us.... When you read a novel it all seems so old and easy, but when you fall in love yourself, then you learn that nobody knows anything, and each must decide for himself.... My dear ones, my sisters... I've confessed, now I shall keep silence.... Like the lunatics in Gogol's story, I'm going to be silent... silent...

[ANDREY enters, followed by FERAPONT.]

ANDREY. *[Angrily]* What do you want? I don't understand.

FERAPONT. *[At the door, impatiently]* I've already told you ten times, Andrey Sergeyevitch.

ANDREY. In the first place I'm not Andrey Sergeyevitch, but sir. *[Note: Quite literally, "your high honour," to correspond to Andrey's rank as a civil servant.]*

FERAPONT. The firemen, sir, ask if they can go across your garden to the river. Else they go right round, right round; it's a nuisance.

ANDREY. All right. Tell them it's all right. *[Exit FERAPONT]* I'm tired of them. Where is Olga? *[OLGA comes out from behind the screen]* I came to you for the key of the cupboard. I lost my own. You've got a little key. *[OLGA gives him the key; IRINA goes behind her screen; pause]* What a huge fire! It's going down now. Hang it all, that Ferapont made me so angry that I talked nonsense to him.... Sir, indeed.... *[A pause]* Why are you so silent, Olga? *[Pause]* It's time you stopped all that nonsense and behaved as if you were properly alive.... You are here, Masha. Irina is here, well, since we're all here, let's come to a complete understanding, once and for all. What have you against me? What is it?

OLGA. Please don't, Audrey dear. We'll talk to-morrow. *[Excited]* What an awful night!

ANDREY. *[Much confused]* Don't excite yourself. I ask you in perfect calmness; what have you against me? Tell me straight.

VERSHININ'S VOICE. Trum-tum-tum!

MASHA. *[Stands; loudly]* Tra-ta-ta! *[To OLGA]* Goodbye, Olga, God bless you. *[Goes behind screen and kisses IRINA]* Sleep well.... Good-bye, Andrey. Go away now, they're tired... you can explain to-morrow.... *[Exit.]*

ANDREY. I'll only say this and go. Just now.... In the first place, you've got something against Natasha, my wife; I've noticed it since the very day of my marriage. Natasha is a beautiful and honest creature, straight and honourable— that's my opinion. I love and respect my wife; understand it, I respect her, and I insist that others should respect her too. I repeat, she's an honest and honourable person, and all your disapproval is simply silly... *[Pause]* In the second place, you seem to be annoyed because I am not a professor, and am not engaged in study. But I work for the zemstvo, I am a member of the district council, and I consider my service as worthy and as high as the service of science. I am a member of the district council, and I am proud of it, if you want to know. *[Pause]* In the third place, I have still this to say... that I have mortgaged the house without obtaining your permission.... For that I am to blame, and ask to be forgiven. My debts led me into doing it... thirty-five thousand... I do not play at cards any more, I stopped long ago, but the chief thing I have to say in my defence is that you girls receive a pension, and I don't... my wages, so to speak.... *[Pause.]*

KULIGIN. *[At the door]* Is Masha there? *[Excitedly]* Where is she? It's queer.... *[Exit.]*

ANDREY. They don't hear. Natasha is a splendid, honest person. *[Walks about in silence, then stops]* When I married I thought we should be happy... all of us.... But, my God.... *[Weeps]* My dear, dear sisters, don't believe me, don't believe me.... *[Exit.]*

[Fire-alarm. The stage is clear.]

IRINA. *[behind her screen]* Olga, who's knocking on the floor?

OLGA. It's doctor Ivan Romanovitch. He's drunk.

IRINA. What a restless night! *[Pause]* Olga! *[Looks out]* Did you hear? They are taking the brigade away from us; it's going to be transferred to some place far away.

OLGA. It's only a rumour.

IRINA. Then we shall be left alone.... Olga!

OLGA. Well?

IRINA. My dear, darling sister, I esteem, I highly value the Baron, he's a splendid man; I'll marry him, I'll consent, only let's go to Moscow! I implore you, let's go! There's nothing better than Moscow on earth! Let's go, Olga, let's go!

Curtain.

ACT IV

[The old garden at the house of the PROSOROVS. There is a long avenue of firs, at the end of which the river can be seen. There is a forest on the far side of the river. On the right is the terrace of the house: bottles and tumblers are on a table here; it is evident that champagne has just been drunk. It is midday. Every now and again passers-by walk across the garden, from the road to the river; five soldiers go past rapidly. CHEBUTIKIN, in a comfortable frame of mind which does not desert him throughout the act, sits in an armchair in the garden, waiting to be called. He wears a peaked cap and has a stick. IRINA, KULIGIN with a cross hanging from his neck and without his moustaches, and TUZENBACH are standing on the terrace seeing off FEDOTIK and RODE, who are coming down into the garden; both officers are in service uniform.]

TUZENBACH. *[Exchanges kisses with FEDOTIK]* You're a good sort, we got on so well together. *[Exchanges kisses with RODE]* Once again.... Good-bye, old man!

IRINA. Au revoir!

FEDOTIK. It isn't au revoir, it's good-bye; we'll never meet again!

KULIGIN. Who knows! *[Wipes his eyes; smiles]* Here I've started crying!

IRINA. We'll meet again sometime.

FEDOTIK. After ten years—or fifteen? We'll hardly know one another then; we'll say, "How do you do?" coldly.... *[Takes a snapshot]* Keep still.... Once more, for the last time.

RODE. *[Embracing TUZENBACH]* We shan't meet again.... *[Kisses IRINA'S hand]* Thank you for everything, for everything!

FEDOTIK. *[Grieved]* Don't be in such a hurry!

TUZENBACH. We shall meet again, if God wills it. Write to us. Be sure to write.

RODE. *[Looking round the garden]* Good-bye, trees! *[Shouts]* Yo-ho! *[Pause]* Good-bye, echo!

KULIGIN. Best wishes. Go and get yourselves wives there in Poland.... Your Polish wife will clasp you and call you "kochanku!" *[Note: Darling]* *[Laughs.]*

FEDOTIK. *[Looking at the time]* There's less than an hour left. Soleni is the only one of our battery who is going on the barge; the rest of us are going with the main body. Three batteries are leaving to-day, another three to-morrow and then the town will be quiet and peaceful.

TUZENBACH. And terribly dull.

RODE. And where is Maria Sergeyevna?

KULIGIN. Masha is in the garden.

FEDOTIK. We'd like to say good-bye to her.

RODE. Good-bye, I must go, or else I'll start weeping.... [*Quickly embraces KULIGIN and TUZENBACH, and kisses IRINA'S hand*] We've been so happy here....

FEDOTIK. [*To KULIGIN*] Here's a keepsake for you... a note-book with a pencil.... We'll go to the river from here.... [*They go aside and both look round.*]

RODE. [*Shouts*] Yo-ho!

KULIGIN. [*Shouts*] Good-bye!

[*At the back of the stage FEDOTIK and RODE meet MASHA; they say good-bye and go out with her.*]

IRINA. They've gone.... [*Sits on the bottom step of the terrace.*]

CHEBUTIKIN. And they forgot to say good-bye to me.

IRINA. But why is that?

CHEBUTIKIN. I just forgot, somehow. Though I'll soon see them again, I'm going to-morrow. Yes... just one day left. I shall be retired in a year, then I'll come here again, and finish my life near you. I've only one year before I get my pension.... [*Puts one newspaper into his pocket and takes another out*] I'll come here to you and change my life radically... I'll be so quiet... so agree... agreeable, respectable....

IRINA. Yes, you ought to change your life, dear man, somehow or other.

CHEBUTIKIN. Yes, I feel it. *[Sings softly.]* "Tarara-boom-deay...."

KULIGIN. We won't reform Ivan Romanovitch! We won't reform him!

CHEBUTIKIN. If only I was apprenticed to you! Then I'd reform.

IRINA. Feodor has shaved his moustache! I can't bear to look at him.

KULIGIN. Well, what about it?

CHEBUTIKIN. I could tell you what your face looks like now, but it wouldn't be polite.

KULIGIN. Well! It's the custom, it's modus vivendi. Our Director is clean-shaven, and so I too, when I received my inspectorship, had my moustaches removed. Nobody likes it, but it's all one to me. I'm satisfied. Whether I've got moustaches or not, I'm satisfied.... *[Sits.]*

[At the back of the stage ANDREY is wheeling a perambulator containing a sleeping infant.]

IRINA. Ivan Romanovitch, be a darling. I'm awfully worried. You were out on the boulevard last night; tell me, what happened?

CHEBUTIKIN. What happened? Nothing. Quite a trifling matter. *[Reads paper]* Of no importance!

KULIGIN. They say that Soleni and the Baron met yesterday on the boulevard near the theatre....

TUZENBACH. Stop! What right... *[Waves his hand and goes into the house.]*

KULIGIN. Near the theatre... Soleni started behaving offensively to the Baron, who lost his temper and said something nasty....

CHEBUTIKIN. I don't know. It's all bunkum.

KULIGIN. At some seminary or other a master wrote "bunkum" on an essay, and the student couldn't make the letters out—thought it was a Latin word "luckum." *[Laughs]* Awfully funny, that. They say that Soleni is in love with Irina and hates the Baron.... That's quite natural. Irina is a very nice girl. She's even like Masha, she's so thoughtful.... Only, Irina your character is gentler. Though Masha's character, too, is a very good one. I'm very fond of Masha. *[Shouts of "Yo-ho!" are heard behind the stage.]*

IRINA. *[Shudders]* Everything seems to frighten me today. *[Pause]* I've got everything ready, and I send my things off after dinner. The Baron and I will be married to-morrow, and to-morrow we go away to the brickworks, and the next day I go to the school, and the new life begins. God will help me! When I took my examination for the teacher's post, I actually wept for joy and gratitude.... *[Pause]* The cart will be here in a minute for my things....

KULIGIN. Somehow or other, all this doesn't seem at all serious. As if it was all ideas, and nothing really serious. Still, with all my soul I wish you happiness.

CHEBUTIKIN. *[With deep feeling]* My splendid... my dear, precious girl.... You've gone on far ahead, I won't catch up with you. I'm left behind like a migrant bird grown old, and unable to fly. Fly, my dear, fly, and God be with you! *[Pause]* It's a pity you shaved your moustaches, Feodor Ilitch.

KULIGIN. Oh, drop it! *[Sighs]* To-day the soldiers will be gone, and everything will go on as in the old days. Say what you will, Masha is a good, honest woman. I love her very much, and thank my fate for her. People have such different fates. There's a Kosirev who works in the excise department here. He was at school with me; he was expelled from the fifth class of the High School for being entirely unable to understand *ut consecutivum*. He's awfully hard up now and in very poor health, and when I meet him I say to him, "How do you do, *ut consecutivum*." "Yes," he says, "precisely *consecutivum*..." and coughs. But I've been successful all my life, I'm happy, and I even have a Stanislaus Cross, of the second class, and now I myself teach others that *ut consecutivum*. Of course, I'm a clever man, much cleverer than many, but happiness doesn't only lie in that....

["The Maiden's Prayer" is being played on the piano in the house.]

IRINA. To-morrow night I shan't hear that "Maiden's Prayer" any more, and I shan't be meeting Protopopov....

[Pause] Protopopov is sitting there in the drawing-room; and he came to-day...

KULIGIN. Hasn't the head-mistress come yet?

IRINA. No. She has been sent for. If you only knew how difficult it is for me to live alone, without Olga.... She lives at the High School; she, a head-mistress, busy all day with her affairs and I'm alone, bored, with nothing to do, and hate the room I live in.... I've made up my mind: if I can't live in Moscow, then it must come to this. It's fate. It can't be helped. It's all the will of God, that's the truth. Nicolai Lvovitch made me a proposal.... Well? I thought it over and made up my mind. He's a good man... it's quite remarkable how good he is.... And suddenly my soul put out wings, I became happy, and light-hearted, and once again the desire for work, work, came over me.... Only something happened yesterday, some secret dread has been hanging over me....

CHEBUTIKIN. Luckum. Rubbish.

NATASHA. *[At the window]* The head-mistress.

KULIGIN. The head-mistress has come. Let's go. *[Exit with IRINA into the house.]*

CHEBUTIKIN. "It is my washing day.... Tara-ra... boom-deay."

[MASHA approaches, ANDREY is wheeling a perambulator at the back.]

MASHA. Here you are, sitting here, doing nothing.

CHEBUTIKIN. What then?

MASHA. *[Sits]* Nothing.... *[Pause]* Did you love my mother?

CHEBUTIKIN. Very much.

MASHA. And did she love you?

CHEBUTIKIN. *[After a pause]* I don't remember that.

MASHA. Is my man here? When our cook Martha used to ask about her gendarme, she used to say my man. Is he here?

CHEBUTIKIN. Not yet.

MASHA. When you take your happiness in little bits, in snatches, and then lose it, as I have done, you gradually get coarser, more bitter. *[Points to her bosom]* I'm boiling in here.... *[Looks at ANDREY with the perambulator]* There's our brother Andrey.... All our hopes in him have gone. There was once a great bell, a thousand persons were hoisting it, much money and labour had been spent on it, when it suddenly fell and was broken. Suddenly, for no particular reason.... Andrey is like that....

ANDREY. When are they going to stop making such a noise in the house? It's awful.

CHEBUTIKIN. They won't be much longer. *[Looks at his watch]* My watch is very old-fashioned, it strikes the hours.... *[Winds the watch and makes it strike]* The first, second, and fifth batteries are to leave at one o'clock precisely. *[Pause]* And I go to-morrow.

ANDREY. For good?

CHEBUTIKIN. I don't know. Perhaps I'll return in a year. The devil only knows... it's all one.... *[Somewhere a harp and violin are being played.]*

ANDREY. The town will grow empty. It will be as if they put a cover over it. *[Pause]* Something happened yesterday by the theatre. The whole town knows of it, but I don't.

CHEBUTIKIN. Nothing. A silly little affair. Soleni started irritating the Baron, who lost his temper and insulted him, and so at last Soleni had to challenge him. *[Looks at his watch]* It's about time, I think.... At half-past twelve, in the public wood, that one you can see from here across the river.... Piff-paff. *[Laughs]* Soleni thinks he's Lermontov, and even writes verses. That's all very well, but this is his third duel.

MASHA. Whose?

CHEBUTIKIN. Soleni's.

MASHA. And the Baron?

CHEBUTIKIN. What about the Baron? *[Pause.]*

MASHA. Everything's all muddled up in my head.... But I say it ought not to be allowed. He might wound the Baron or even kill him.

CHEBUTIKIN. The Baron is a good man, but one Baron more or less—what difference does it make? It's all the same! *[Beyond the garden somebody shouts "Co-ee! Hallo! "]*

You wait. That's Skvortsov shouting; one of the seconds. He's in a boat. *[Pause.]*

ANDREY. In my opinion it's simply immoral to fight in a duel, or to be present, even in the quality of a doctor.

CHEBUTIKIN. It only seems so.... We don't exist, there's nothing on earth, we don't really live, it only seems that we live. Does it matter, anyway!

MASHA. You talk and talk the whole day long. *[Going]* You live in a climate like this, where it might snow any moment, and there you talk.... *[Stops]* I won't go into the house, I can't go there.... Tell me when Vershinin comes.... *[Goes along the avenue]* The migrant birds are already on the wing.... *[Looks up]* Swans or geese.... My dear, happy things.... *[Exit.]*

ANDREY. Our house will be empty. The officers will go away, you are going, my sister is getting married, and I alone will remain in the house.

CHEBUTIKIN. And your wife?

[FERAPONT enters with some documents.]

ANDREY. A wife's a wife. She's honest, well-bred, yes; and kind, but with all that there is still something about her that degenerates her into a petty, blind, even in some respects misshapen animal. In any case, she isn't a man. I tell you as a friend, as the only man to whom I can lay bare my soul. I love Natasha, it's true, but sometimes she seems extraordinarily vulgar, and then I lose myself and can't understand why I love her so much, or, at any rate, used to love her....

CHEBUTIKIN. *[Rises]* I'm going away to-morrow, old chap, and perhaps we'll never meet again, so here's my advice. Put on your cap, take a stick in your hand, go... go on and on, without looking round. And the farther you go, the better.

[SOLENI goes across the back of the stage with two officers; he catches sight of CHEBUTIKIN, and turns to him, the officers go on.]

SOLENI. Doctor, it's time. It's half-past twelve already. *[Shakes hands with ANDREY.]*

CHEBUTIKIN. Half a minute. I'm tired of the lot of you. *[To ANDREY]* If anybody asks for me, say I'll be back soon.... *[Sighs]* Oh, oh, oh!

SOLENI. "He didn't have the time to sigh. The bear sat on him heavily." *[Goes up to him]* What are you groaning about, old man?

CHEBUTIKIN. Stop it!

SOLENI. How's your health?

CHEBUTIKIN. *[Angry]* Mind your own business.

SOLENI. The old man is unnecessarily excited. I won't go far, I'll only just bring him down like a snipe. *[Takes out his scent-bottle and scents his hands]* I've poured out a whole bottle of scent to-day and they still smell... of a dead body. *[Pause]* Yes.... You remember the poem

"But he, the rebel seeks the storm,
As if the storm will bring him rest..."?

CHEBUTIKIN. Yes.

"He didn't have the time to sigh,
The bear sat on him heavily."

[Exit with SOLENI.]

[Shouts are heard. ANDREY and FERAPONT come in.]

FERAPONT. Documents to sign....

ANDREY. *[Irritated].* Go away! Leave me! Please! *[Goes away with the perambulator.]*

FERAPONT. That's what documents are for, to be signed. *[Retires to back of stage.]*

[Enter IRINA, with TUZENBACH in a straw hat; KULIGIN walks across the stage, shouting "Co-ee, Masha, co-ee!"]

TUZENBACH. He seems to be the only man in the town who is glad that the soldiers are going.

IRINA. One can understand that. *[Pause]* The town will be empty.

TUZENBACH. My dear, I shall return soon.

IRINA. Where are you going?

TUZENBACH. I must go into the town and then... see the others off.

IRINA. It's not true... Nicolai, why are you so absentminded to-day? *[Pause]* What took place by the theatre yesterday?

TUZENBACH. *[Making a movement of impatience]* In an hour's time I shall return and be with you again. *[Kisses her hands]* My darling... *[Looking her closely in the face]* it's five years now since I fell in love with you, and still I can't get used to it, and you seem to me to grow more and more beautiful. What lovely, wonderful hair! What eyes! I'm going to take you away to-morrow. We shall work, we shall be rich, my dreams will come true. You will be happy. There's only one thing, one thing only: you don't love me!

IRINA. It isn't in my power! I shall be your wife, I shall be true to you, and obedient to you, but I can't love you. What can I do! *[Cries]* I have never been in love in my life. Oh, I used to think so much of love, I have been thinking about it for so long by day and by night, but my soul is like an expensive piano which is locked and the key lost. *[Pause]* You seem so unhappy.

TUZENBACH. I didn't sleep at night. There is nothing in my life so awful as to be able to frighten me, only that lost key torments my soul and does not let me sleep. Say something to me *[Pause]* say something to me....

IRINA. What can I say, what?

TUZENBACH. Anything.

IRINA. Don't! don't! *[Pause.]*

TUZENBACH. It is curious how silly trivial little things, sometimes for no apparent reason, become significant. At first you laugh at these things, you think they are of no importance, you go on and you feel that you haven't got the strength to stop yourself. Oh don't let's talk about it! I am happy. It is as if for the first time in my life I see these firs, maples, beeches, and they all look at me inquisitively and wait. What beautiful trees and how beautiful, when one comes to think of it, life must be near them! *[A shout of Co-ee! in the distance]* It's time I went.... There's a tree which has dried up but it still sways in the breeze with the others. And so it seems to me that if I die, I shall still take part in life in one way or another. Good-bye, dear.... *[Kisses her hands]* The papers which you gave me are on my table under the calendar.

IRINA. I am coming with you.

TUZENBACH. *[Nervously]* No, no! *[He goes quickly and stops in the avenue]* Irina!

IRINA. What is it?

TUZENBACH. *[Not knowing what to say]* I haven't had any coffee to-day. Tell them to make me some.... *[He goes out quickly.]*

[IRINA stands deep in thought. Then she goes to the back of the stage and sits on a swing. ANDREY comes in with the perambulator and FERAPONT also appears.]

FERAPONT. Andrey Sergeyevitch, it isn't as if the documents were mine, they are the government's. I didn't make them.

ANDREY. Oh, what has become of my past and where is it? I used to be young, happy, clever, I used to be able to think and frame clever ideas, the present and the future seemed to me full of hope. Why do we, almost before we have begun to live, become dull, grey, uninteresting, lazy, apathetic, useless, unhappy.... This town has already been in existence for two hundred years and it has a hundred thousand inhabitants, not one of whom is in any way different from the others. There has never been, now or at any other time, a single leader of men, a single scholar, an artist, a man of even the slightest eminence who might arouse envy or a passionate desire to be imitated. They only eat, drink, sleep, and then they die... more people are born and also eat, drink, sleep, and so as not to go silly from boredom, they try to make life many-sided with their beastly backbiting, vodka, cards, and litigation. The wives deceive their husbands, and the husbands lie, and pretend they see nothing and hear nothing, and the evil influence irresistibly oppresses the children and the divine spark in them is extinguished, and they become just as pitiful corpses and just as much like one another as their fathers and mothers.... *[Angrily to FERAPONT]* What do you want?

FERAPONT. What? Documents want signing.

ANDREY. I'm tired of you.

FERAPONT. *[Handing him papers]* The hall-porter from the law courts was saying just now that in the winter there were two hundred degrees of frost in Petersburg.

ANDREY. The present is beastly, but when I think of the future, how good it is! I feel so light, so free; there is a light in the distance, I see freedom. I see myself and my children freeing ourselves from vanities, from kvass, from goose baked with cabbage, from after-dinner naps, from base idleness....

FERAPONT. He was saying that two thousand people were frozen to death. The people were frightened, he said. In Petersburg or Moscow, I don't remember which.

ANDREY. *[Overcome by a tender emotion]* My dear sisters, my beautiful sisters! *[Crying]* Masha, my sister....

NATASHA. *[At the window]* Who's talking so loudly out here? Is that you, Andrey? You'll wake little Sophie. *Il ne faut pas faire du bruit, la Sophie est dormée deja. Vous êtes un ours.* *[Angrily]* If you want to talk, then give the perambulator and the baby to somebody else. Ferapont, take the perambulator!

FERAPONT. Yes'm. *[Takes the perambulator.]*

ANDREY. *[Confused]* I'm speaking quietly.

NATASHA. *[At the window, nursing her boy]* Bobby! Naughty Bobby! Bad little Bobby!

ANDREY. *[Looking through the papers]* All right, I'll look them over and sign if necessary, and you can take them back to the offices....

[Goes into house reading papers; FERAPONT takes the perambulator to the back of the garden.]

NATASHA. *[At the window]* Bobby, what's your mother's name? Dear, dear! And who's this? That's Aunt Olga. Say to your aunt, "How do you do, Olga!"

[Two wandering musicians, a man and a girl, are playing on a violin and a harp. VERSHININ, OLGA, and ANFISA come out of the house and listen for a minute in silence; IRINA comes up to them.]

OLGA. Our garden might be a public thoroughfare, from the way people walk and ride across it. Nurse, give those musicians something!

ANFISA. *[Gives money to the musicians]* Go away with God's blessing on you. *[The musicians bow and go away]* A bitter sort of people. You don't play on a full stomach. *[To IRINA]* How do you do, Arisha! *[Kisses her]* Well, little girl, here I am, still alive! Still alive! In the High School, together with little Olga, in her official apartments... so the Lord has appointed for my old age. Sinful woman that I am, I've never lived like that in my life before.... A large flat, government property, and I've a whole room and bed to myself. All government property. I wake up at nights and, oh God, and Holy Mother, there isn't a happier person than I!

VERSHININ. *[Looks at his watch]* We are going soon, Olga Sergeyevna. It's time for me to go. *[Pause]* I wish you every... every.... Where's Maria Sergeyevna?

IRINA. She's somewhere in the garden. I'll go and look for her.

VERSHININ. If you'll be so kind. I haven't time.

ANFISA. I'll go and look, too. *[Shouts]* Little Masha, co-ee! *[Goes out with IRINA down into the garden]* Co-ee, co-ee!

VERSHININ. Everything comes to an end. And so we, too, must part. *[Looks at his watch]* The town gave us a sort of farewell breakfast, we had champagne to drink and the mayor made a speech, and I ate and listened, but my soul was here all the time.... *[Looks round the garden]* I'm so used to you now.

OLGA. Shall we ever meet again?

VERSHININ. Probably not. *[Pause]* My wife and both my daughters will stay here another two months. If anything happens, or if anything has to be done...

OLGA. Yes, yes, of course. You need not worry. *[Pause]* To-morrow there won't be a single soldier left in the town, it will all be a memory, and, of course, for us a new life will begin.... *[Pause]* None of our plans are coming right. I didn't want to be a head-mistress, but they made me one, all the same. It means there's no chance of Moscow....

VERSHININ. Well... thank you for everything. Forgive me if I've... I've said such an awful lot—forgive me for that too, don't think badly of me.

OLGA. *[Wipes her eyes]* Why isn't Masha coming...

VERSHININ. What else can I say in parting? Can I philosophize about anything? *[Laughs]* Life is heavy. To many of us it seems dull and hopeless, but still, it must be acknowledged that it is getting lighter and clearer, and it seems that the time is not far off when it will be quite clear. *[Looks at his watch]* It's time I went! Mankind used to be absorbed in wars, and all its existence was filled with campaigns, attacks, defeats, now we've outlived all that, leaving after us a great waste place, which there is nothing to fill with at present; but mankind is looking for something, and will certainly find it. Oh, if it only happened more quickly. *[Pause]* If only education could be added to industry, and industry to education. *[Looks at his watch]* It's time I went....

OLGA. Here she comes.

[Enter MASHA.]

VERSHININ. I came to say good-bye....

[OLGA steps aside a little, so as not to be in their way.]

MASHA. *[Looking him in the face]* Good-bye. *[Prolonged kiss.]*

OLGA. Don't, don't. *[MASHA is crying bitterly]*

VERSHININ. Write to me.... Don't forget! Let me go.... It's time. Take her, Olga Sergeyevna... it's time... I'm late...

[He kisses OLGA'S hand in evident emotion, then embraces MASHA once more and goes out quickly.]

OLGA. Don't, Masha! Stop, dear.... *[KULIGIN enters.]*

KULIGIN. *[Confused]* Never mind, let her cry, let her.... My dear Masha, my good Masha.... You're my wife, and I'm happy, whatever happens... I'm not complaining, I don't reproach you at all.... Olga is a witness to it. Let's begin to live again as we used to, and not by a single word, or hint...

MASHA. [Restraining her sobs] "There stands a green oak by the sea,

> And a chain of bright gold is around it....
> And a chain of bright gold is around it...."

I'm going off my head... "There stands... a green oak... by the sea."...

OLGA. Don't, Masha, don't... give her some water....

MASHA. I'm not crying any more....

KULIGIN. She's not crying any more... she's a good... [A shot is heard from a distance.]

MASHA.

> "There stands a green oak by the sea,
> And a chain of bright gold is around it...
> An oak of green gold...."

I'm mixing it up.... [Drinks some water] Life is dull... I don't want anything more now... I'll be all right in a moment.... It doesn't matter.... What do those lines mean? Why do they run in my head? My thoughts are all tangled.

[IRINA enters.]

OLGA. Be quiet, Masha. There's a good girl.... Let's go in.

MASHA. *[Angrily]* I shan't go in there. *[Sobs, but controls herself at once]* I'm not going to go into the house, I won't go....

IRINA. Let's sit here together and say nothing. I'm going away to-morrow.... *[Pause.]*

KULIGIN. Yesterday I took away these whiskers and this beard from a boy in the third class.... *[He puts on the whiskers and beard]* Don't I look like the German master.... *[Laughs]* Don't I? The boys are amusing.

MASHA. You really do look like that German of yours.

OLGA. *[Laughs]* Yes. *[MASHA weeps.]*

IRINA. Don't, Masha!

KULIGIN. It's a very good likeness....

[Enter NATASHA.]

NATASHA. *[To the maid]* What? Mihail Ivanitch Protopopov will sit with little Sophie, and Andrey Sergeyevitch can take little Bobby out. Children are such a bother.... *[To IRINA]* Irina, it's such a pity you're going away to-morrow. Do stop just another week. *[Sees KULIGIN and screams; he laughs and takes off his beard and whiskers]* How you frightened me! *[To IRINA]* I've grown used to you and do you think it will be easy for me to part from you? I'm going to have Andrey and his violin put into your room—let him fiddle away in there!—and we'll put little Sophie into his room. The beautiful, lovely child! What a little girlie! To-day she looked at me with such pretty eyes and said "Mamma!"

KULIGIN. A beautiful child, it's quite true.

NATASHA. That means I shall have the place to myself to-morrow. *[Sighs]* In the first place I shall have that avenue of fir-trees cut down, then that maple. It's so ugly at nights.... *[To IRINA]* That belt doesn't suit you at all, dear.... It's an error of taste. And I'll give orders to have lots and lots of little flowers planted here, and they'll smell.... *[Severely]* Why is there a fork lying about here on the seat? *[Going towards the house, to the maid]* Why is there a fork lying about here on the seat, I say? *[Shouts]* Don't you dare to answer me!

KULIGIN. Temper! temper! *[A march is played off; they all listen.]*

OLGA. They're going.

[CHEBUTIKIN comes in.]

MASHA. They're going. Well, well.... Bon voyage! *[To her husband]* We must be going home.... Where's my coat and hat?

KULIGIN. I took them in... I'll bring them, in a moment.

OLGA. Yes, now we can all go home. It's time.

CHEBUTIKIN. Olga Sergeyevna!

OLGA. What is it? *[Pause]* What is it?

CHEBUTIKIN. Nothing... I don't know how to tell you.... *[Whispers to her.]*

OLGA. *[Frightened]* It can't be true!

CHEBUTIKIN. Yes... such a story... I'm tired out, exhausted, I won't say any more.... *[Sadly]* Still, it's all the same!

MASHA. What's happened?

OLGA. *[Embraces IRINA]* This is a terrible day... I don't know how to tell you, dear....

IRINA. What is it? Tell me quickly, what is it? For God's sake! *[Cries.]*

CHEBUTIKIN. The Baron was killed in the duel just now.

IRINA. *[Cries softly]* I knew it, I knew it....

CHEBUTIKIN. *[Sits on a bench at the back of the stage]* I'm tired.... *[Takes a paper from his pocket]* Let 'em cry.... *[Sings softly]* "Tarara-boom-deay, it is my washing day...." Isn't it all the same!

[The three sisters are standing, pressing against one another.]

MASHA. Oh, how the music plays! They are leaving us, one has quite left us, quite and for ever. We remain alone, to begin our life over again. We must live... we must live....

IRINA. *[Puts her head on OLGA's bosom]* There will come a time when everybody will know why, for what purpose, there is all this suffering, and there will be no more mysteries. But now we must live... we must work, just work! To-morrow, I'll go away alone, and I'll teach and give my whole life to those who, perhaps, need it. It's autumn now, soon it will be winter, the snow will cover everything, and I shall be working, working....

OLGA. *[Embraces both her sisters]* The bands are playing so gaily, so bravely, and one does so want to live! Oh, my God! Time will pass on, and we shall depart for ever, we shall be forgotten; they will forget our faces, voices, and even how many there were of us, but our sufferings will turn into joy for those who will live after us, happiness and peace will reign on earth, and people will remember with kindly words, and bless those who are living now. Oh dear sisters, our life is not yet at an end. Let us live. The music is so gay, so joyful, and, it seems that in a little while we shall know why we are living, why we are suffering.... If we could only know, if we could only know!

[The music has been growing softer and softer; KULIGIN, smiling happily, brings out the hat and coat; ANDREY wheels out the perambulator in which BOBBY is sitting.]

CHEBUTIKIN. *[Sings softly]* "Tara... ra-boom-deay.... It is my washing-day."... *[Reads a paper]* It's all the same! It's all the same!

OLGA. If only we could know, if only we could know!

Curtain.

Made in the USA
Las Vegas, NV
14 July 2023